883.
01
HOM
BLO

Homer.

WITHDRAWN

COMPREHENSIVE RESEARCH
AND STUDY GUIDE

Homer

BLOOM'S
MAJOR
POETS

EDITED AND WITH AN INTRODUCTION
BY HAROLD BLOOM

CURRENTLY AVAILABLE

BLOOM'S MAJOR SHORT STORY WRITERS

Anton Chekhov

Joseph Conrad

Stephen Crane

William Faulkner

F. Scott Fitzgerald

Nathaniel Hawthorne

Ernest Hemingway

O. Henry

Shirley Jackson

Henry James

James Joyce

D. H. Lawrence

Jack London

Herman Melville

Flannery O'Connor

Edgar Allan Poe

Katherine Anne Porter

J. D. Salinger

John Steinbeck

Mark Twain

John Updike

Eudora Welty

BLOOM'S MAJOR WORLD POETS

Maya Angelou

Robert Browning

Geoffrey Chaucer

Samuel T. Coleridge

Dante

Emily Dickinson

John Donne

T. S. Eliot

Robert Frost

Homer

Langston Hughes

John Keats

John Milton

Sylvia Plath

Edgar Allan Poe

Poets of World War I

Shakespeare's Poems & Sonnets

Percy Shelley

Alfred, Lord Tennyson

Walt Whitman

William Wordsworth

William Butler Yeats

Homer

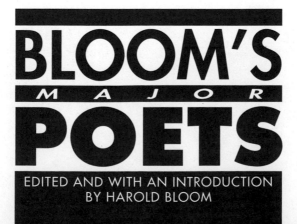

BLOOM'S *MAJOR* POETS

EDITED AND WITH AN INTRODUCTION
BY HAROLD BLOOM

© 2001 by Chelsea House Publishers, a subsidiary of
Haights Cross Communications.

Introduction © 2001 by Harold Bloom.

Printed and bound in the United States of America.

First Printing
1 3 5 7 9 8 6 4 2

Library of Congress Cataloging-in-Publication Data
applied for:

ISBN 0-7910-5938-3

Chelsea House Publishers
1974 Sproul Road, Suite 400
Broomall, PA 19008-0914

The Chelsea House World Wide Web address is
http://www.chelseahouse.com

Contributing Editor: Emmy Chang

Produced by: Robert Gerson Publisher's Services, Santa Barbara, CA

Contents

User's Guide

This volume is designed to present biographical, critical, and bibliographical information on the author's best-known or most important poems. Following Harold Bloom's editor's note and introduction is a detailed biography of the author, discussing major life events and important literary accomplishments. A thematic and structural analysis of each poem follows, tracing significant themes, patterns, and motifs in the work.

A selection of critical extracts, derived from previously published material from leading critics, analyzes aspects of each poem. The extracts consist of statements from the author, if available, early reviews of the work, and later evaluations up to the present. A bibliography of the author's writings (including a complete list of all books written, cowritten, edited, and translated), a list of additional books and articles on the author and the work, and an index of themes and ideas in the author's writings conclude the volume.

∼

Harold Bloom is Sterling Professor of the Humanities at Yale University and Henry W. and Albert A. Berg Professor of English at the New York University Graduate School. He is the author of over 20 books, including *Shelley's Mythmaking* (1959), *The Visionary Company* (1961), *Blake's Apocalypse* (1963), *Yeats* (1970), *A Map of Misreading* (1975), *Kabbalah and Criticism* (1975), *Agon: Toward a Theory of Revisionism* (1982), *The American Religion* (1992), *The Western Canon* (1994), and *Omens of Millennium: The Gnosis of Angels, Dreams, and Resurrection* (1996). *The Anxiety of Influence* (1973) sets forth Professor Bloom's provocative theory of the literary relationships between the great writers and their predecessors. His most recent books include *Shakespeare: The Invention of the Human,* a 1998 National Book Award finalist, and *How to Read and Why,* which was published in 2000.

Professor Bloom earned his Ph.D. from Yale University in 1955 and has served on the Yale faculty since then. He is a 1985 MacArthur Foundation Award recipient, served as the Charles Eliot Norton Professor of Poetry at Harvard University in 1987–88, and has received honorary degrees from the universities of Rome and Bologna. In 1999, Professor Bloom received the prestigious American Academy of Arts and Letters Gold Medal for Criticism.

Currently, Harold Bloom is the editor of numerous Chelsea House volumes of literary criticism, including the series BLOOM'S NOTES, BLOOM'S MAJOR DRAMATISTS, BLOOM'S MAJOR NOVELISTS, MAJOR LITERARY CHARACTERS, MODERN CRITICAL VIEWS, MODERN CRITICAL INTERPRETATIONS, and WOMEN WRITERS OF ENGLISH AND THEIR WORKS.

Editor's Note

My Introduction contrasts Achilles, childlike and doom-eager hero, with the very different Odysseus, experientially mature and a survivor-of-survivors.

As there are twenty-six Critical Views represented in this volume, half each on the *Iliad* and the *Odyssey*, I will confine myself here to mentioning only a few that are among the most useful.

Milman Parry, the father of modern Homeric scholarship, illuminates the epithet, center of oral composition, while Bruno Snell shows us how different Homeric man is from our sense of the human.

Adam Parry, Milman Parry's son, brilliantly examines the language of Achilles, after which Jasper Griffin teaches us what it means that the Homeric gods serve as audience for the protagonists of the *Iliad.*

W. B. Stanford explores the ambiguities of Odysseus, while Anne Amory, Adam Parry's wife, shrewdly analyzes the psychology of Odysseus and his wife, Penelope.

Hugh Lloyd-Jones sketches the parameters of moral fable in the *Odyssey,* after which Andrew Ford crucially demonstrates how Homer must battle against his own sense of belatedness in poetic tradition. ❀

Introduction

We do not know whether Homer was one man or two, or perhaps the name for a school of bards, a tradition of storytellers who chanted the *Iliad* and the *Odyssey* aloud to rapt audiences. And yet whoever edited and revised the two epics into their current form was himself a genius, who not only organized the two great poems, but very likely also composed more of them than modern scholarly fashion is able to admit. Oral composition evidently relied upon inherited formulae, but listen to the differences when two of your friends retell the same story, one of them being far more articulate and imaginative than the other. Perhaps Homer was essentially a traditional bard, and certainly a latecomer, with an anxious relationship to earlier poets. And yet a contemporary reader confronts the two great epic poems as rather imposing unities, and not a medley of voices.

In his admirable *Homer: The Poetry of the Past* (1992), Andrew Ford emphasizes that Homer, a professional "singer," gave us a book, or books, whether he himself wrote or dictated to a scribe:

> . . . as readers we will interpret; but in doing so we may remember that we are listening not to that original and indifferent choir or even to its first echoes in early Ionia, but to a book, a format for storing singing that changed singing forever.

Myself a literary critic approaching seventy, I think of Homer and the Bible, Dante and Shakespeare, Proust and James Joyce, as *books.* Technology—I am warned—will make books obsolete, though I doubt that computers also will change singing forever. In any case, we are not returning to an oral culture, however we transmit our texts in the future. And I am not altogether persuaded that the experience of reading the Homeric epics is enormously enhanced by constantly reminding ourselves that oral traditions were crucial in their composition.

Most scholars believe that the *Odyssey* reached its final form later than the *Iliad* did, and there are lines in the *Odyssey* that seem to parody remarkable lines in the *Iliad*. Though the epics are very different, they could have been assembled by the same poet-editor, perhaps at opposite ends of a long life. We do not know, and it may be better not to know. It fascinates me that the *Odyssey* became more influential than the *Iliad* in the nineteenth and twentieth centuries. Achilles has obsessed writers much less than Odysseus/Ulysses has, once Western culture became Post-Enlightenment. Tennyson's "Ulysses" is a superb dramatic monologue, while Joyce's *Ulysses* is the dominant prose fiction in English of its century. It would be difficult to imagine an "Achilles" by Tennyson, or a vaster *Achilles* by James Joyce. As the West has developed a more acute sense of cultural belatedness, it has turned away from Achilles to Ulysses. The *Iliad* seems more remote from us than the *Odyssey*, almost as though the story of the wrath of Achilles is Classical, and that of Ulysses' return to Penelope is Romantic. Such impressions are illusory, yet pragmatically they enforce themselves. Both poems are surpassingly harsh, and yet the heroism of Achilles seems more tragic, and the resourcefulness of Odysseus (to give him back his Greek name) both more comic and more a model for us.

Aesthetically, our estrangement from the *Iliad* can be said to heighten the epic's effect upon us; the poem's power is enhanced by distancing, and challenges us to break with over-familiarities. Like its descendent, Milton's *Paradise Lost,* the *Iliad* requires mediation if we are to understand it fully, but even a partial apprehension of this difficult splendor is an overwhelming experience. Achilles's fury transcends its occasion, and impresses us as a protest against mortality, paradoxically manifested by a frenzy for battle. Here is Achilles shouting his ecstasy for slaughter, as rendered by Tennyson with an eloquence and intensity worthy of the original:

> Then rose Æakidês dear to Zeus; and round
> The Warrior's puissant shoulders Pallas flung
> Her fringèd ægis, and around his head
> The glorious goddess wreathed a golden cloud,
> And from it lighted an all-shining flame.
> As when a smoke from a city goes to heaven
> Far off from out an island girt by foes,
> All day the men contend in grievous war
> From their own city, but with set of sun
> Their fires flame thickly, and aloft the glare
> Flies streaming, if perchance the neighbours round
> May see, and sail to help them in the war;
> So from his head the splendour went to heaven.
> From wall to dyke he stept, he stood, not joined
> The Achæans—honouring his wise mother's word—
> There standing, shouted, and Pallas far away
> Called; and a boundless panic shook the foe.

For like the clear voice when a trumpet shrills,
Blown by the fierce beleaguerers of a town,
So rang the clear voice of Æakidês;
And when the brazen cry Æakidês
Was heard among the Trojans, all their hearts
Were troubled, and the full-maned horses whirled
The chariots backward, knowing griefs at hand;
And sheer-astounded were the charioteers
To see the dread, unweariable fire
That always o'er the great Peleion's head
Burned, for the bright-eyed goddess made it burn.
Thrice from the dyke he sent his mighty shout,
Thrice backward reeled the Trojans and allies;
And there and then twelve of their noblest died
Among their spears and chariots.

Achilles (Æakidês in Tennyson's spelling) and Pallas Athena shout in response to one another, and Athena creates a nimbus of fire about his head.

The war-cries and flame in conjunction stun the Trojans, and in themselves kill a dozen heroes. This astonishing passage is profoundly representative of the *Iliad*, and can serve as a token of the sublime otherness of the poem.

We are hardly at home in the *Odyssey*, and yet despite all the marvels we are more at ease with it than with the angry splendors of the *Iliad*, "the poem of force," as Simone Weil termed it. There is violence enough in the *Odyssey*, but Odysseus never resorts to force until the resources of his guile are exhausted. Achilles, though he frightens and awes us, is childlike at best, childish in his sulkings, but Odysseus, mature from his start, becomes wiser as his poem unfolds. Samuel Butler, sage author of *The Way of All Flesh*, argued that the *Odyssey* must have been written by a woman. Emulating Butler nearly a century later, I suggested that *The Book of J*, the oldest strand of the Pentateuch, also may have been a woman's work, on internal grounds not altogether dissimilar from Butler's. The ironies of the *Odyssey*, like those of the Yahwist text, suggest a wise woman's awareness of male limits and of divine caprice.

Athena comes to Odysseus when he most needs her, though her relationship to the wanderer is never quite as familial as it was with the half-divine Achilles. Achilles, whose story ends in the *Iliad* with his killing of Hector, in a sense is granted completion by the *Odyssey*, as part of its program of never repeating an incident from the *Iliad*. The poet-editor of the *Odyssey* presumably knew the *Iliad* as a written work, set down in a form essentially final, unless we are to assume a singer's memory of more-than-Talmudic proportions. That is not impossible, though unlikely. The *Odyssey* is respectfully wary of the *Iliad*, though frequently quite sly in its allusions and parodies. Whereas the agonistic spirit dominates the *Iliad*, Odysseus strives always for survival and returning home, and not to be the best of all the Achaeans. In Hades, Agamemnon assures Achilles that his fame and his monument exceed those of any other hero, whereas Odysseus flees his fame wherever it would further compound his already enormous difficulties in getting home.

Poseidon, god of the sea, is the implacable opponent of Odysseus, which presents the hero with extraordinary difficulties in returning to his island kingdom. To evade the rule of Poseidon requires a hero very different from Achilles. Odysseus' name has a curious double meaning: either to be an avenger who contaminates others with a curse, or to be oneself the curse's victim. That makes Odysseus a dangerous figure, both to himself and to everyone else. Though he is at last triumphant in his quest, nevertheless he is exiled from home, by war and by wandering, for twenty years. He is an arch troublemaker, even when he wills otherwise, yet he must escape both the war and the sea, as well as aspects of his perpetual effect upon all he encounters.

Odysseus, as I once wrote, is even more a storyteller than he is a quester, and his story always concerns his own survival. Survivors interest readers quite intensely; because of our common mortality, we identify ourselves with survivors. Odysseus may be termed the archetypal survivor: realistic, pragmatic, hardened, more than a little cold, totally mature, endlessly curious, and cunning beyond all measure. One sees why writers after Homer transformed Odysseus into a villain: Pindar, Sophocles, Euripides, Virgil, and (more equivocally) Dante and Shakespeare (in *Troilus and Cressida*). It is important to separate these later versions of Odysseus/Ulysseus from the indubitable hero of the *Odyssey*.

Odysseus, in Homer's epic, undergoes a complex development, as R. B. Rutherford argues. The hero gains in severe self-control, and in his sense of the motives of everyone he encounters. He thus acquires a qualified moral authority, despite his continued wiliness, greed, vanity, and his genius for telling lies about himself. This becomes crucial in his triumph over the suitors of Penelope, where his heroism is directly aided by Athena. Yet his heroic agon to assert and to reestablish his identity is very much his own enterprise. Is there another fictive hero, before the great Shakespearean protagonists, who so massively and influentially triumphs in forging and in affirming unmistakable identity? ❀

Biography of
Homer

"All men's thoughts," said Xenophanes, "have been shaped by Homer from the beginning." And yet, despite his centrality in Western thought, we know almost nothing substantive of the life of Homer. Though authorship of the Greek epics has historically been assigned to one shadowy figure, there even now remains no scholarly consensus as to whether Homer composed the *Iliad*, the *Odyssey*, or both; whether he invented, or merely edited, older tale-cycles; whether he was one man, or two men, or a whole tradition of singers—or a woman.

Even in antiquity the mystique surrounding Homer was so great that at least seven ancient Greek cities vied for the honor of having been his birthplace. Aristotle called their author "in the serious style the poet of poets," but the epics' significance ranged even further. The *Iliad* and *Odyssey* codified heroic ideals, and also comprised the Greeks' principal source—along with Hesiod's *Theogony*—of knowledge of the gods. Even long after the decline of Greece itself, the Homeric epics would continue to form the mainstay of Western education and scholarship.

Archaeological records indicate that Troy did fall, possibly to Mycenaeans who were in turn conquered by Dorians. Herodotus sets the date at about 1250 B.C., and, with Thucydides, believes Homer to have lived in the ninth century B.C. Not only the Doric invasion, but the Ionian colonization as well, would thus separate the poet from his subject. Indeed, Homer's tales, though treating a heroic long-ago age, employ relatively modern trappings in the telling. The world in Achilleus' shield, for instance—and in the extended, or "Homeric," similes—borrows scenes and culture not from the 13th century, when Troy fell, but from the ninth.

Though the earliest traditions favor single authorship, since the 18th century, in the wake of F. A. Wolf's *Prolegomena ad Homerum* (1795), debate has raged over the question of who "Homer" actually was. Wolf founded the "Analyst" school, which held the epics to be a compendium of older and younger story layers. Such a structure would account for at least some of the innumerable internal contradictions in both poems.

Homeric scholarship was dominated by quarrels between Analysts and their opponents—the "Unitarians," who favored single authorship—until Milman Parry's groundbreaking work in the 1920s. Supporting his claims with impressively rigorous textual analysis, Parry argued that the epics developed organically through a tradition of oral composers. Relying on both memory and improvisation, these singers continually modified and added to the poems with every new performance. (Parry and Albert Bates Lord, among others, eventually pursued field research among tribes still practicing oral techniques in segments of Yugoslavia, and their conclusions seemed to confirm this theory.) It is estimated that of the two poems' 28,000 lines, some 2,000 recur at least once: counting recurrences, nearly one-fifth of the text therefore consists of repeated lines. Parry contended that the itinerant bards who sang the poems used such formulas and epithets as mnemonic devices. His thesis could also explain the key role in the poem of ring structure, a narrative form in which the poet continually interrupts himself to open new digressions, each of which is nested within the last.

The *Iliad* and *Odyssey* are composed in dactylic hexameter, in a blend of dialects that seems to show special familiarity with the Ionic and Aeolic areas of the coast of Asia Minor. They may have assumed their present form when normalized for a performance at the Panathenaea, in the sixth century B.C.; and are believed to have been given their present form of 24 book-divisions around the third century B.C., possibly by Aristarchus of Samothrace.

There are significant differences between the two works. Different words are often used for common objects in the two poems, and the poems themselves vary considerably in tone and scope. Where the *Iliad* achieves a towering sublimity with a simple plot, the *Odyssey* weaves a necklace of stories out of unrelated folktales, producing something more closely akin to the modern idea of a novel. The *Odyssey* presupposes the *Iliad*, but never alludes specifically to any of its events. It contains far fewer similes, and has in some respects more moral preoccupations than the *Iliad*. In it the heroic code, too, has undergone some modification. For instance, Achilleus had been indisputably the hero of the prior poem; and while his status as such is not now questioned, still we are apprised that it is the cunning of Odysseus' wooden horse that actually brought down Troy. The

Achilleus of the *Odyssey* has, moreover, repented his choice in the *Iliad*, and tells Odysseus it is better "to break sod as a farm hand [. . .] than lord it over all the exhausted dead."

Such deviations have led some to believe that the *Odyssey* dates from a later era, one with altered standards of nobility and greatness. Unitarians have typically accounted for discrepancies of this kind by suggesting that the *Odyssey* was composed much later in the poet's life. Longinus famously called the *Iliad* the work of mid-day, the *Odyssey* a setting sun which "preserves its original splendor and majesty though derived of its meridian heat."

Erich Auerbach remarked that Homer narrated events in a tone "not even passion could disturb." In functions of plot, on the other hand, the epics are surprisingly advanced. Aristotle, notably, praised the skillfulness of both poems: they are not confined to an obviously linear story-line, but show an extremely sophisticated mastery of such devices as flashbacks and dramatic irony.

We are, by now, too far removed in time for the "Homeric question" ever to be decisively settled. Nevertheless, whatever the epics'—or their author's—true history, the *Iliad* and *Odyssey* may indisputably be said to have inaugurated the literature of the West. ❀

Thematic Analysis of
the *Iliad*

In the Greek, the *Iliad* announces its subject in the very first word: *mênis*. The larger history of Troy is refracted through the prism of Achilleus' *mênis*, or wrath; thus the narrative can be confined to a mere four days, and the Judgment of Paris granted only an elliptical three lines [XXIV: 28–30]. Nor do we need to be told of the end of Troy, for the *Iliad* is the war in miniature. An entire city falls when Hektor dies.

Despite the surgical fascination of some of its battle scenes, the epic's savage ballet ultimately centers more on killing than on wounding: its focus is less on warfare than it is on death. Much of the *Iliad*'s sublime tone flows from its hypnotic accumulation of necrologues; these are in turn tempered by the disconcerting delicacy of its imagery, in particular in the extended similes. By juxtaposing the balance of battle with the figure of a poor woman weighing wool [XII. 433–35], for instance, or in comparing an eye impaled on Peneleos' spear with "the head of a poppy" [XIV. 499], the poem continually recalls us to a world not at war, infusing with pathos what would otherwise have been a mere catalogue of death.

Moreover, as Rachel Bespaloff wrote, "The philosophy of the *Iliad* excludes resentment." Homer steeps his poem in war and suffering, but glorifies or deplores neither. They are, in the heroic code, merely a fact of life.

Book I opens with the Achaians in the grip of a plague, sent by Apollo to punish Agamemnon's refusal of Chryses' ransom for his daughter Chryseis. Agamemnon is now willing to give the girl up, but demands that another battle-prize be found, "lest I only / among the Argives go without, since that were unfitting."

Achilleus reminds Agamemnon, reasonably enough, that the prizes have all been distributed, and he can be recompensed after the defeat of the Trojans. The quarrel escalates, however, as Agamemnon threatens to take Achilleus' own concubine, Briseis. Achilleus is only stayed from murder when Athene seizes his hair; he vows in fury to withdraw from the fighting. Nestor tries to make peace, but no peace can be had: to Agamemnon, Achilleus is only a warrior; to Achilleus, Agamemnon is only a king.

Achilleus calls on his mother, the goddess Thetis, for justice, and she exacts from Zeus a promise of help for the Trojans, to avenge the dishonor of her son. Zeus begins by sending a false dream advising Agamemnon to attack [**Book II**]. With characteristically poor judgment, Agamemnon decides first to test his men by suggesting they return home. His plan backfires, for the men are only too willing to go, and the Achaians remain only by the persuasion of Odysseus. There then follows the catalogue of ships, a panoramic display of nearly 300 lines enumerating the tribes that have come to the war at Troy. At a command from Zeus, Hektor in turn marshals his troops, motivating a parallel list of the Trojan forces.

Paris comes forward from the Trojan ranks [**Book III**], but retreats on catching sight of Menelaos. Rebuked for his cowardice by Hektor, he agrees to a single combat with Menelaos to settle the war for good. Meanwhile, the gods' messenger Iris summons Helen to witness the battle. Troy's elders marvel at her approach, finding it little wonder nations should go to war for a beauty such as hers. Priam, the Trojan king, speaks kindly to Helen, and she identifies for him (and for the reader) a number of the Achaian heroes, including Agamemnon, Odysseus, and Aias.

Though sealed with a sacrifice, the terms of the duel are not to be fulfilled, for as Menelaos is on the point of defeating Paris, Aphrodite appears in a *deus ex machina* and spirits him away. Helen initially refuses to join Paris in his bedchamber, but the goddess threatens Helen until she relents. (Helen is, notably, the only character in the *Iliad* other than Achilleus ever to flout the will of a god.) The Achaians declare Menelaos the victor by forfeit.

Back at Olympus, Zeus proposes a compromise between the pro-Achaian and pro-Trojan factions. Hera and Athene will not be satisfied, however, and at Athene's urging, the Trojan Pandaros fires an unprovoked shot at Menelaos in **Book IV**. Before long full-scale battle is again underway.

The Achaian Diomedes rises to prominence in an *aristeia*, or period of sustained heroism in combat [**Books V** and **VI**], even wounding Aphrodite as she carries the injured Aineias to safety. This is also the scene of the encounter between Diomedes and Glaukos in which ephemeral human life is compared to the generation of leaves, in a trope that will recur throughout Western literature. The combatants' discovery that their families are bound by friendship and a resulting exchange of gifts is balanced by a wry observation that Glaukos has had the worse end of the deal in trading his gold armor for Diomedes' bronze.

Bespaloff called Hektor "the guardian of the perishable joys," and nowhere is this more apparent than in his meeting with his wife and child in this book. The battle helmet, which frightens the baby Astyanax, connects the hero's world of war with Andromache's sphere of domesticity, heightening the pathos of the events at Troy. Hektor's words to Andromache repeat exactly those of Agamemnon in Book IV: "For I know this thing well in my heart, and my mind knows it: / there will come a day when sacred Ilion shall perish . . ." E. R. Dodds characterized the Greek culture as turned by shame rather than by guilt, and we have a clear illustration of this here: Troy's greatest warrior remains, not out of passionate conviction, but because abandoning the war would be shameful.

Hektor issues an open challenge to single combat [**Book VII**], but only after Nestor reproaches their cowardice do nine of the Greeks come forward. Lots are drawn and Aias is selected to fight the Trojan champion, but their battle ends indecisively with nightfall.

The Greeks resolve to build a wall around their camp— inexplicably, in this ninth year of the war. To the message that Paris will forfeit the treasures he carried off but not Helen herself, Diomedes replies that neither will be taken back now: the Achaians will not go until Troy has been destroyed.

Zeus forbids intervention on the part of the gods [**Book VIII**], in a ban that will not be lifted formally until late in the epic. At Nestor's advice, an embassy is sent to propitiate Achilleus [**Book IX**]. Odysseus enumerates the gifts Agamemnon has offered, among them restitution of the untouched Briseis and his own daughter's hand in marriage. Odysseus further appeals to Achilleus' loyalty to the Achaians, and reminds him of the glory to be won by killing Hektor. Achilleus dismisses these lures, however: he has come to question the heroic code, seeing how little glory profits the winner.

Fate has offered Achilleus the alternatives of either a short, heroic life, or a long, peaceful obscurity. Though his choice is sometimes considered to animate the *Iliad*, it is never again referred to: as Martin Mueller observes, it is not that Achilleus has failed to make a decision, but that he flirts with unmaking it. He now swears that only when Hektor fires the Achaian ships will he return to the war.

Book X, the "Doloneia," is believed by commentators to be a later addition, as its events do not advance the plot in the slightest. In it Diomedes and Odysseus make a foray into the Trojan camp, meeting the spy Dolon, whom they question and kill. At the camp, Diomedes kills 13 of the sleeping men while Odysseus steals Rhesos' horses, the Trojans' best.

Agamemnon has his *aristeia* [**Book XI**], gaining an advantage for the Achaians. But Zeus sends a promise that once Agamemnon has been wounded, the tide will turn and Hektor will be allowed to kill unimpeded until dark. The Greeks retreat with the wounding of Diomedes and Odysseus, and Zeus continues to favor the Trojan advance.

Book XII culminates in the smashing of the Achaian gate by Hektor. As elsewhere in the epic, special stress is laid on the stature of warriors in the heroic past; not two men "of men such as men are now," could lift the stone he wields.

With Zeus' attention elsewhere, Poseidon violates the moratorium [**Book XIII**], intervening in favor of the Achaians. When the Lokrian archers overwhelm the Trojans, Hektor, counseled by Poulydamas, sounds a retreat.

Diomedes, Odysseus, and Agamemnon now confer with Nestor [**Book XIV**]. A cry sent up by Poseidon inspires the Achaians with courage, and Hera plots the seduction of Zeus in order to distract him. She first tricks Aphrodite into lending her girdle to her, then enlists Sleep's aid with a bribe. Zeus' words in this scene strongly echo Paris' address to Helen in Book III.

With Zeus no longer watching the battle, Hektor is wounded by Aias, and Poseidon helps drive the Trojans back. Zeus eventually wakes, however [**Book XV**], and threatens to punish Hera for her deceit.

The battle is now joined, with Zeus protecting Hektor even to the extent of knocking a bow out of Teukros' hands. Patroklos appeals to Achilleus to help the Greeks [**Book XVI**] or, failing that, to lend him his armor with which to frighten the Trojans—a gambit first suggested by Nestor in Book X. Achilleus, unwilling to renege on his vow, nevertheless lends the armor. He directs Patroklos, however, to retreat once the Trojans have been repulsed. Meanwhile Hektor has reached the water, and the first of the ships is fired at last.

Following an impressive *aristeia*, Patroklos, encouraged by Zeus, disregards Achilleus' warning and is struck down by Apollo himself, along with Euphorbos and Hektor. Hektor puts on Achilleus' armor [**Book XVII**], and there is a prolonged battle for the body of Patroklos.

Antilochus breaks the news of Patroklos' death to Achilleus [**Book XVIII**], who swears vengeance on Hektor. Thetis reminds her son that his own death will soon follow, but he remains firm. The sight and war cry of Achilleus is enough to terrify the Trojans, and the Greeks recover Patroklos' body. But Hector overrules Poulydamas' prudent recommendation of retreat, for Hector, filled with pride over the defeat of Patroklos, believes he may defeat Achilleus.

Achilleus promises Patroklos Hektor's armor and head, and as well the sacrifice of 12 Trojans. Thetis meanwhile visits Hephaistos, who forges for her the new armor and shield of Achilleus. These are described at length in a celebrated *ekphrasis*.

Thetis brings the arms to Achilleus [**Book XIX**], and Achilleus and Agamemnon formally reconcile. Achilleus is eager to return to the fray, but the more prudent Odysseus counsels the taking of food and drink, and Agamemnon insists on the promised gifts be brought. Since the battle is made uneven with Achilleus' return, Zeus now lifts the ban on divine intervention in the war [**Book XX**]. Much of the fighting then resembles a chess match, as various gods favor specific Trojans or Achaians.

Achilleus' *aristeia* is the *Iliad*'s most impressive. He rejects the supplication of Lykaon [**Book XXI**] and even defies the god of the river Xanthos, whose waters are choked with the corpses the Greek warrior has made. The gods are now openly in contest with one another, but their struggles seem frivolous beside the exploits of Achilleus. The *aristeia* continues unabated until Apollo, impersonating Agenor, draws Achilleus from the fighting so the Trojans can retreat within the city.

Against the entreaties of Priam and Hekabe [**Book XXII**], Hektor waits valiantly as Achilleus approaches. At the last moment, however, he loses his nerve and runs. Zeus weighs out their portions of death, and Hektor's sinks; after Hektor runs three laps around the city, Athene tricks him into stopping. At last realizing he is doomed, Hektor nevertheless resolves to die valiantly. His death is marked with almost exactly the same lines as those that heralded the death of Patroklos. Achilleus begins the defilement of Hektor's corpse, dragging it through the dust behind his chariot.

Mourning continues for Patroklos [**Book XXIII**], and the promised sacrifices are duly made. His rage unabated, Achilleus continues to desecrate Hektor's corpse, though to no avail, for Apollo and Aphrodite protect the body.

The funeral games for Patroklos which follow permit a glimpse of Achilleus in his proper element, as a prelude to his civilized decision of **Book XXIV.** At last Zeus orders Achilleus to accept Priam's ransom. Iris is sent to inform Priam, who is escorted for part of his journey by the disguised Hermes.

Priam begs pity of Achilleus, recalling him to his father Peleus. In rejecting Hektor's pleas in Book XXII, the hero had denied they could share anything, comparing them to men and lions, or wolves and lambs, which "forever . . . hold feelings of hate for each other." Priam's appeal to a common humanity now moves Achilleus, however, and he tells in his turn the parable of the jars of good and evil. To some Zeus grants lives only of ill, he says, to others mixed good and ill; but no human life is free of suffering. His speech echoes Priam's in form and diction, concurring with the king's verdict of a shared fate: "we live in unhappiness, but the gods themselves have no sorrows." To encourage Priam to join him in taking food, Achilleus will further tell the story of Niobe, who remembered to eat despite her grief. That we are fated to die, observed James M. Redfield, "Priam and Achilles recognize in their shared mourning. But the fate of the species is also to live, and this they recognize in their shared meal."

Eleven days of peace are set for the mourning and burial of Hektor. The epic draws to a close with burial rites and feasting; after which, we understand, the armies will go back down into war.

Gilbert Murray observed of the *Iliad* that "the subject is second-rate"; and, of its hero, that "sulking is not a noble, nor yet a poetical, state of mind." And he is right: Achilleus does sulk. When he has been despoiled of one thing, he feels he has been despoiled of everything; his is a child's outrage, single-minded and ruthless. Achilleus' flaw exists, however, not in contradiction to his heroism, but as an outgrowth to it: the violence of his emotions causes his incapacity to think or act in anything but extremes. Achilleus' limits are the limits of the heroic code, and he is as much a monument to its glories and tragedies as is the *Iliad* itself. Even his flaw is noble.

The poet-author of the *Odyssey* pointedly re-centered the Greek victory on Odysseus, the man of reason, and away from Achilleus, the noble warrior: Not strength or arm or swiftness of foot but the cunning of the wooden horse finally takes the citadel of Troy. The heroic code may seem outmoded by history, and even Homer wrote with the consciousness that his warriors had walked in a day long past. But in its austere portrayal of the trap of mortal existence, and in the purity of its hero who is more than a man if not quite a god, the *Iliad* remains permanently unsurpassed. ❀

Critical Views on
the *Iliad*

GOTTHOLD EPHRAÏM LESSING ON EKPHRASIS AND
HELEN OF TROY

[Gotthold Ephraïm Lessing (1729–1781) was a German
dramatist and critic whose plays include *Minna von
Barnhelm* (1767) and *Nathan the Wise* (1779). In this
extract from *Laocoön, or The Limits of Painting and Poetry*
(1766), he shows why physical objects are necessarily
difficult to render in poetic language. He then considers
Homer's methods of describing—or not describing—
everything from weapons and armor to "the face that
launched a thousand ships."]

Homer, I find, paints nothing but continuous actions, and all bodies,
all single things, he paints only by their share in those actions, and in
general only by one feature. ⟨. . .⟩

   A ship is to him now the black ship, now the hollow ship, now the
swift ship, at most the well-rowed black ship. Beyond that he does
not enter on a picture of the ship. But certainly of the navigating, the
putting to sea, the disembarking of the ship, he makes a detailed
picture, one from which the painter must make five or six separate
pictures if he would get it in its entirety upon his canvas. ⟨. . .⟩

   ⟨Homer⟩ will distribute this picture in a sort of story of the object,
in order to let its parts, which we see side by side in Nature, follow in
his painting after each other and as it were keep step with the flow of
the narrative. For instance, he would paint for us the bow of
Pandarus—a bow of horn, of such and such a length, well polished,
and mounted with gold plate at the extremities. How does he
manage it? Does he count out before us all these properties dryly
one after the other? Not at all; that would be to sketch, to make a
copy of such a bow, but not to paint it. He begins with the chase of
the deer, from the horns of which the bow was made; Pandarus had
waylaid and killed it amongst the crags; the horns were of
extraordinary length, and so he destined them for a bow; they are
wrought, the maker joins them, mounts them, polishes them. And
thus, as we have already said, with the poet we see arising what with
the painter we can only see as already arisen. ⟨. . .⟩

Physical beauty arises from the harmonious effect of manifold parts that can be taken in at one view. It demands also that these parts shall subsist side by side; and as things whose parts subsist side by side are the proper subject of painting, so it, and it alone, can imitate physical beauty. The poet, who can only show the elements of beauty one after another, in succession, does on that very account forbear altogether the description of physical beauty, as beauty. He recognises that those elements, arranged in succession, cannot possibly have the effect which they have when placed side by side; that the concentrating gaze which we would direct upon them immediately after their enumeration still affords us no harmonious picture; that it passes the human imagination to represent to itself what kind of effect this mouth, and this nose, and these eyes together have if one cannot recall from Nature or art a similar composition of such features.

Here, too, Homer is the pattern of all patterns. He says: "Nireus was beautiful; Achilles was more beautiful still; Helen possessed a divine beauty." But nowhere does he enter upon the more circumstantial delineation of those beauties. For all that, the poem is based on the beauty of Helen. How greatly would a modern poet have luxuriated in the theme!

True, a certain Constantinus Manasses tried to adorn his bald chronicle with a picture of Helen. I must thank him for the attempt. For really I should hardly know where else I could get hold of an example from which it might more obviously appear how foolish it is to venture something which Homer has so wisely forborne. ⟨. . .⟩

Let us recall the passage where Helen steps into the assembly of the Elders of the Trojan people. The venerable old men looked on her, and one said to the other:—

Οὐ νέμεσις Τρῶας καὶ ἐϋκνήμιδας Ἀχαιοὺς
Τοιῇδ' ἀμφὶ γυναικὶ πολὺν χρόνον ἄλγεα πάσχειν·
Αἰνῶς ἀθανάτῃσι θεῇς εἰς ὦπα ἔοικεν.

What can convey a more vivid idea of Beauty than to have frigid age confessing her well worth the war that has cost so much blood and so many tears? What Homer could not describe in its component parts, he makes us feel in its working. Paint us, then, poet, the satisfaction, the affection, the love, the delight, which beauty produces, and you have painted beauty itself.

—Gotthold Ephraïm Lessing, *Laocoön, Nathan the Wise and Minna von Barnhelm*, William A. Steel, trans. (London: J. M. Dent, 1930): pp. 56, 59–60, 74, 79.

JOHN RUSKIN ON THE GODS

[John Ruskin (1819–1900) was a writer, critic, and lecturer whose works include *Modern Painters* (1848) and *The Stones of Venice* (1851). In this extract he argues against the assumption that Homer could only have intended the gods of the *Iliad* as allegories, maintaining instead that they are both solid and true to life.]

I do not believe that the idea ever weakens itself down to mere allegory. When Pallas is said to attack and strike down Mars, it does not mean merely that Wisdom at that moment prevailed against Wrath. It means that there are, indeed, two great spirits, one entrusted to guide the human soul to wisdom and chastity, the other to kindle wrath and prompt to battle. It means that these two spirits, on the spot where, and at the moment when, a great contest was to be decided between all that they each governed in man, then and there (assumed) human form, and human weapons, and did verily and materially strike at each other, until the Spirit of Wrath was crushed. ⟨. . .⟩

When Juno beats Diana about the ears with her own quiver, for instance, we start at first, as if Homer could not have believed that they were both real goddesses. But what should Juno have done? Killed Diana with a look? Nay, she neither wished to do so, nor could she have done so, by the very faith of Diana's goddess-ship. Diana is as immortal as herself. Frowned Diana into submission? But Diana has come expressly to try conclusions with her, and will by no means be frowned into submission. Wounded her with a celestial lance? That sounds more poetical, but it is in reality partly more savage and partly more absurd, than Homer. More savage, for it makes Juno more cruel, therefore less divine; and more absurd, for it only seems elevated in tone, because we use the word "celestial," which means nothing. What sort of a thing is a "celestial" lance? Not a wooden one. Of what then? Of moonbeams, or clouds, or mist. Well, therefore, Diana's arrows were of mist too; and her quiver, and herself, and Juno, with her lance, and all, vanish into mist. Why not have said at once, if that is all you mean, that two mists met, and one drove the other back? That would have been rational and intelligible, but not to talk of celestial lances. Homer had no such misty fancy; he believed the two goddesses were there in true bodies, with true weapons, on the true earth; and still I ask, what should Juno have done? Not beaten Diana? No; for it is unlady-like. Un-English-lady-like, yes; but by no means un-Greek-lady-like, nor even un-natural-lady-like. If a modern lady does *not* beat her servant or her rival about the ears, it is oftener because she is too weak, or too proud, than because she is of purer mind than Homer's Juno. She will not strike them; but she will overwork the one or slander the other without pity; and Homer would not have thought that one whit more goddess-like than striking them with her open hand.

If, however, the reader likes to suppose that while the two goddesses in personal presence thus fought with arrow and quiver, there was also a broader and vaster contest supposed by Homer between the elements they ruled; and that the goddess of the heavens, as she struck the goddess of the moon on the flushing cheek, was at the same instant exercising omnipresent power in the heavens themselves, and gathering clouds, with which, filled with the moon's own arrows or beams, she was encumbering and concealing the moon; he is welcome to this outcarrying of the idea, provided that he does not pretend to make it an interpretation instead of a mere extension, nor think to explain away my real, running, beautiful beaten Diana, into a moon behind clouds.

—John Ruskin, Modern Painters (London: George Allen, 1904): pp. 226, 228–29.

MILMAN PARRY ON THE EPITHET

[Milman Parry was Associate Professor of Greek at Harvard University and author of *L'Epithète traditionnelle dans Homère* (1928) and *Les Formules et la métrique d'Homère*

(1928). His research drew attention to the importance of formulas and greatly clarified our understanding of the structures of oral epic. Homer often assigns descriptives to meet the demands of a line's meter; Parry here shows how such "fixed" epithets are intended less to define a particular hero than to define and elevate the entire poem.]

Why is the name of Agamemnon used in the nominative case as often as the name of Patroclus, but seven times more often with an epithet? Because he is the commander-in-chief of the Achaean army? Why then does Diomedes in the nominative case appear without an epithet only once out of 42 times, whereas out of an equal number of occurrences Agamemnon in the nominative appears without epithet twelve times? Again why does Menelaus, fine warrior that he was, but clearly no Achilles or Odysseus, deserve the epithet four times as often as they? ⟨. . .⟩

Metrical convenience alone can explain these differing proportions; and therefore we must abandon the idea which offers itself so naturally to us that the courage or the majesty of a hero or a god led the poet to attribute the epithet to him more often. Anyone inclined to believe that Homer chose an epithet in a given passage in order to honour a particular character, will have to concede that, far from indicating the virtues and the deserts of his heroes and gods, the poet has actually falsified our conception of their character. Surely Homer did not believe, as the use of the epithets would suggest, that Menelaus was a braver warrior than Achilles or even Ajax, or that Diomedes surpassed Ajax, or that Patroclus merited fewer titles of honour than any other hero. ⟨. . .⟩

For ⟨Homer⟩ and for his audience alike, the fixed epithet did not so much adorn a single line or even a single poem, as it did the entirety of heroic song. ⟨. . .⟩

δῖος, ⟨. . .⟩ confined to a single hero will not have the same meaning as δῖος applied to many heroes. The former will refer to an individual character; the latter will refer only to a quality of the hero, to one of the several traits which distinguish ordinary men from those of the mythic and marvellous world of the bards. In other words, we must learn to choose between 'divine, and therefore a hero' and 'divine, as other heroes are not'. If, in Homer, δῖος were said only of Odysseus or Achilles, we should have to take it more or less in the sense of θεῖος in the Alexandrian epigram:

πρῶτος δ' εἴς τε θεὸν καὶ ἐς οὐρανὸν ὄμμα τανύσσας,
θεῖε Πλάτων, ἤθη καὶ βίον ηὐγάσαο.

The author of this epigram calls Plato *divine* because he wants us to understand that here was a philosopher whose works and whose life revealed a kind of divinity which did not belong to other philosophers. This is how we must understand πολύμητις and πολύτλας of Odysseus, and πόδας ὠκύς and ποδάρκης of Achilles. The two epithets of Odysseus, used only of him, tell us that he was a man of extraordinary ingenuity and that in the course of his life he experienced extraordinary suffering. The two epithets of Achilles, though they would seem to refer to a part of the legend not dramatized in the *Iliad* and possibly not known to Homer, ascribe to his hero a swiftness of foot unmatched by other heroes. But if we find that Homer applied the epithet δῖος to heroes who differ too much among themselves in rank, prowess, and character for us to conceive of some 'divinity' common to all of them but not shared by other heroes, we shall have to reject for this word the distinctive meaning which comes so naturally to the mind of the modern reader, and is so appropriate to the Alexandrian epigram.

The same is true of μεγαλήτορος, ἀμύμων, θεοειδής, δαΐφρων, and of all other Homeric epithets denoting an abstract quality. If they are used of one hero only, we must see in them the designation of a particular feature; if they are used indifferently for all heroes, we can see in them no more than the designation of a characteristic feature of the generic hero.

—Milman Parry, *The Making of Homeric Verse*, Adam Parry, ed. (London: Oxford University Press, 1971): pp. 136–37, 145–46.

C. M. Bowra on Homer as Poet of a Post-Heroic Age

[C. M. Bowra (1898–1971) was a Fellow at Wadham College, Oxford. His writings include *Greek Lyric Poetry from Alcman to Simonides* (1936), *The Romantic Imagination* (1949), and *From Virgil to Milton* (1957). In this extract from *Tradition and Design in the Iliad* (1930) he notes that, unlike most early epics, the *Iliad* makes no attempt to romanticize death. By exalting heroic ideals without yielding to nihilism, it thus asserts a philosophy of tragedy but not defeat.]

Homer found the subject of the *Iliad* in the doings of an age of heroes. For him the world had changed since those spacious days, and the race of the heaven-born had perished. The world of his similes is different from the world of his story, and he is fully conscious that his contemporaries are weaker than the great men of old. ⟨...⟩

⟨L⟩ying as he does outside the actual age of heroes, he has modified the heroic point of view in some directions, and here he is sharply distinguished from the writers of early Teutonic or French epic. In other early epics honour is all that matters, and defeat is nothing compared with it. The result is a magnificent sense of ultimate failure, which is of no importance provided death be found gloriously against overwhelming odds. The *Fight at Maldon* is a glorification of defeat, and the *Song of Roland* ends on a note of unwearying struggle against unconquerable forces. The *Edda* poems are full of the same proud spirit. Sigurd, Gudrun, Brynhild are in turn beaten and brought to disaster. But the *Iliad* is not like these. Even in the death of Hector, a theme worthy of early Germanic poetry, we do not feel a savage exultation in death just because it is glorious. Homer feels differently, and he makes defeat more tragic than glorious. Hector's death is an irreparable loss. It means the fall of Troy, the enslavement of Andromache, the misery of Astyanax. The pitiful side of it is what concerns Homer even more than the heroic. Hector dies magnificently, but his glory is no comfort to his defenceless family and friends. ⟨...⟩

The famous words of Glaucus are only a prelude to a tale of Bellerophon's heroism, and this is the key to Homer's attitude. It is the heroism that matters, and man being mortal has more chance of glory than the immortal gods. The only real pessimist in the *Iliad* is Achilles, who doubts the value of heroism, and complains that in the end the brave man and the idler find the same fate. But Achilles is the victim of passion, even of obsession, and his despair is part of his lapse from true nobility. Hector provides the right corrective to him. In the beautiful scene with Andromache he is not deluded by any false hopes of the future. But he never falters in his conviction that what he does is the right thing to do. Even when Achilles pursues him with certain death, in his moment of doubt and indecision he knows that it is best to face his adversary and kill him or be killed. This is not the decision of a desperate man, but of one who knows what his task is and does not shrink from it. What holds for Hector holds for the other heroes. From none of them goes up the cry that their efforts are to no purpose and not worth making. The absence of this note of despair is remarkable. In their different ways both Sophocles and Euripides at times give way to it. It is the burden of some of the finest words written by Shakespeare and by Pindar. It is the cry of Cassandra as she goes to her doom in the *Agamemnon*, and of Macbeth when he hears that his wife is dead. But in the *Iliad* for all its sorrow and suffering this despair hardly exists.

—C. M. Bowra, *Tradition and Design in the Iliad* (Westport: Greenwood Press, 1977): pp. 234, 235–36, 248–49.

Bruno Snell on Homeric Man

[Bruno Snell (1896–1986) was Rector of the University of Hamburg and author of *Poetry and Society (1961)* and *The Discovery of the Mind* (1953). Here he suggests that, in attributing all changes of mind to the influence of external gods, Homer provides for no true notion of a divided self. Homeric psychology may thus be seen as an intermediary step in the evolution of our understanding of consciousness.]

Quantity, not intensity, is Homer's standard of judgment. ⟨In Book XXIV⟩ Priam laments the fate of Hector: 'I groan and brood over countless griefs'. πολλὰ αἰτεῖν, πολλὰ ὀτρύνειν, 'to demand much', 'to exhort much' is a frequent figure, even where the act of demanding or exhorting takes place only once. Our 'much' offers a similar ambiguity. Never does Homer, in his descriptions of ideas or emotions, go beyond a purely spatial or quantitative definition; never does he attempt to sound their special, non-physical nature. As far as he is concerned, ideas are conveyed through the *noos*, a mental organ which in turn is analogous to the eye; consequently 'to know' is ἐιδέναι which is related to ἰδεῖν 'to see', and in fact originally means 'to have seen'. The eye, it appears, serves as Homer's model for the absorption of experiences. From this point of view the intensive coincides with the extensive: he who has seen much sufficiently often possesses intensive knowledge. ⟨. . .⟩

Homer is not even acquainted with intensity in its original sense, as 'tension'. A tension within the soul has no more reality for him than a tension in the eye would, or a tension in the hand. Here too the predicates of the soul remain completely within the bounds set for physical organs. There are no divided feelings in Homer; not until Sappho are we to read of the bitter-sweet Eros. Homer is unable to say: 'half-willing, half-unwilling;' instead he says: 'he was willing, but his *thymos* was not'. This does not reflect a contradiction within one and the same organ, but the contention between a man and one of his organs; we should compare our saying: 'my hand desired to reach out, but I withdrew it'. Two different things or substances engage in a quarrel with one another. As a result there is in Homer no genuine reflexion, no dialogue of the soul with itself. ⟨. . .⟩

Whenever a man accomplishes, or pronounces, more than his previous attitude had led others to expect, Homer connects this, in so far as he tries to supply an explanation, with the interference of a god. It should be noted especially that Homer does not know genuine personal decisions; even where a hero is shown pondering two alternatives the intervention of the gods plays the key role. This divine meddling is, of course, a necessary complement of Homer's notions regarding the human mind and the soul. The *thymos* and the *noos* are so very little different from other physical organs that they cannot very well be looked upon as a genuine source of impulses; the πρῶτον κινοῦν, Aristotle's 'first mover', is hidden from Homer's ken, as is the concept of any vital centre which controls the organic system. Mental and spiritual acts are due to the impact of external factors, and man is the open target of a great many forces which impinge on him, and penetrate his very core. That is the reason why Homer has so much to say about forces, why, in fact, he has so many words for our term 'force': μένος, σθένος, βίη, κῖκυς, ἴς, κράτος, ἀλκή, δύναμις. ⟨. . .⟩

Homeric man has not yet awakened to the fact that he possesses in his own soul the source of his powers, but neither does he attach the forces to his person by means of magical practices; he receives them as a natural and fitting donation from the gods.

—Bruno Snell, *The Discovery of the Mind: The Greek Origins of European Thought*, T. G. Rosenmeyer, trans. (Cambridge, Mass.: Harvard University Press, 1953): pp. 18, 19, 20, 21.

Adam Parry on Heroic Language and the Wrath of Achilleus

[Adam Parry (1928–1972) was Assistant Professor of Greek at Yale University. His works include *Logos and Ergon in Thucydides* (1981) and *The Language of Achilles* (1989). Below, Parry uses the fire imagery of Book VIII to show that heroic language is fundamentally uniform in its descriptions of the world. Since Achilleus no longer shares the common code of that language or that world, the poet is faced with finding a new way for him to speak.]

The feeling of this passage ⟨Book VIII, lines 553–65⟩ is that the multitude of Trojan watchfires is something marvellous and brilliant, that fills the heart with gladness. But this description, we remember, comes at the point in the story when the situation of the Achaeans is for the first time obviously perilous; and it is followed by the 9th book, where Agamemnon in desperation makes his extravagant and vain offer to Achilles, if he will save the army. The imminent disaster of the Achaeans is embodied in these very fires. Yet Homer pauses in the dramatic trajectory of his narrative to represent not the horror of the fires, but their glory. I suggest that this is due precisely to the formulaic language he employs. There is a single best way to describe a multitude of shining fires; there are established phrases, each with its special and economical purpose, to compose such a description. Homer may arrange these with consummate art; but the nature of his craft does not incline him, or even allow, him to change them, or in any way to present the particular dramatic significance of the fires in this situation. Instead, he presents the constant qualities of all such fires.

The formulaic character of Homer's language means that everything in the world is regularly presented as all men (all men within the poem, that is) commonly perceive it. The style of Homer emphasizes constantly the accepted attitude toward each thing in the world, and this makes for a great unity of experience. ⟨. . .⟩

Achilles is ⟨. . .⟩ the one Homeric hero who does not accept the common language, and feels that it does not correspond to reality. But what is characteristic of the *Iliad*, and makes it unique as a tragedy, is that this otherness of Achilles is nowhere stated in clear and precise terms. Achilles can only say, "There was, after all, no grace in it," or ask questions that cannot really be answered: "But why should the Argives be fighting against the Trojans?" or make demands that can never be satisfied: ". . . until he pays back all my heart-rending grief." ⟨. . .⟩

Achilles has no language with which to express his disillusionment. Yet he expresses it, and in a remarkable way. He does it by misusing the language he disposes of. He asks questions that cannot be answered and makes demands that cannot be met. He uses conventional expressions where we least expect him to, as when he speaks to Patroclus in book 16 of a hope of being offered material gifts by the Greeks, when we know that he has been offered these gifts and that they are meaningless to him; or as when he says that he has won great glory by slaying Hector, when we know that he is really fighting to avenge his comrade, and that he sees no value in the glory that society can confer. ⟨. . .⟩ Achilles' tragedy, his final isolation, is that he can in no sense, including that of language (unlike, say, Hamlet), leave the society which has become alien to him. And Homer uses the epic speech a long poetic tradition gave him to transcend the limits of that speech.

—Adam Parry, "The Language of Achilles," *Transactions and Proceedings of the American Philological Association* 87 (1956): pp. 2–3, 6–7.

DIETER LOHMANN ON RING COMPOSITION AND THE CHARIOT RACE

[Dieter Lohmann is the author of *Die Andromache-Szenen der Ilias* (1988) and *Kalypso bei Homer und James Joyce* (1998). In this essay on "The 'Inner Composition' of the Speeches in the *Iliad*" (1970), he analyzes one of the most prominent examples of Homeric "ring structure," Nestor's speech to Antilochus in Book XXIII. Nestor's argument, as Lohmann demonstrates, not only describes but effectively *becomes* a chariot race, mimicking in form the race's own pattern of moving to a point, pivoting, then circling back.]

The next speech with strictly executed ring composition is probably the most extensive example of this kind in the *Iliad*: 23. 306–48. Achilles has opened the funeral games in honour of the dead Patroclus and the charioteers line up for the race, among them Antilochus, Nestor's son. Then the old father steps up to Antilochus and makes a speech comprising no fewer than 43 verses in which he gives his son detailed tactical advice for the contest. Outside this self-contained passage, however, are the three introductory verses 306–8 in which Nestor praises his son for his knowledge of chariot racing. So, he says, it would actually be unnecessary to instruct him. Nevertheless Nestor does not miss the opportunity to demonstrate his didactic prowess.

23. 306–48:	The paraphrase:
306–8	Introduction.
a 309–12	Pessimism.
	For you know well how to steer around the turning-post but your horses are the slowest. So I am pessimistic about the result. But though the others' horses are swifter, they themselves are not as intelligent as you.
b 313–18	Act with intelligence!
	Come on, my dear son, bring your cunning intelligence (=*metis*) to bear so that the prizes will not elude you. Through *metis* the woodcutter achieves more than through strength. Through *metis* the helmsman steers the ship. Through *metis* one charioteer surpasses another.

c	319–25	General characterization of the charioteer.
1.	319–21	Negative:
		He who simply trusts his horses and chariot will weave from side to side without purpose, the horses will drift off course, he will not be able to control them.
2.	322–5	Positive:
		But he who has worse horses but knows the 'tricks' will watch the turning-post and turn round it tightly and will not forget to hold a steady course but will steer unswervingly and watch the chariot ahead.
d	326–33	Elaborate description of the turning-post.
c′	334–43a	Practical instructions.
1.	334–40a	Positive:
		Drive the team close to the turning-post and lean to the left of the car. Spur on the right-hand horse, give him full rein. The left-hand horse must graze the turning-post so that the wheel hub seems to touch the side.
2.	340b–3a	Negative:
		But avoid touching it so that you do not injure your horses and break your chariot to the joy of the others, and your own disgrace.
b′	343b	But, my dear son, act with foresight!
a′	344–8	Optimism.
		Once you have passed the turning point, no one will catch you up, even if he were driving the godlike Arion, Adrastus' horse which had divine origins, or Laomedon's horses. ⟨. . .⟩

Here a new aspect of ring composition comes to light and in the 'archaic' poet it is a surprising one. Nestor's speech does not, like a didactic lecture, simply *describe* the process of a chariot race at the critical phase when one drives round the turning-post but in the way it is composed *it becomes* a chariot race:

a:	The situation before the turn. Its pessimism is psychologically sound: I am pessimistic, the horses of the others are faster.

b c d c′ b′:	The process of turning, visually clearly composed, and, in the centre, that around which everything 'turns', the turning-post.
a′:	The situation after the turn: nothing can now go wrong, even if the others had Arion!

The subject-matter determines the form: the composition becomes a programme. Ring composition in the image of the chariot race: driving there—turn—driving back. We see a bridging of a period of time and through it the connection of time of action and time of narrative.

—Dieter Lohmann, "The 'Inner Composition' of the Speeches in the *Iliad*" (1970), in *Homer: German Scholarship in Translation*, G. M. Wright and P. V. Jones, eds. (Oxford: Oxford University Press, 1997): pp. 74–76, 77.

JAMES M. REDFIELD ON DOGS IN THE *ILIAD*

[James M. Redfield is a professor of Classical Languages at the University of Chicago and author of *Nature and Culture in the* Iliad (1975). In this extract he shows how dogs represent an aspect of the warrior that both is, and is required to be, permanently uncivilized. As an image of impurity, the dog thus reflects the epic's strong ambivalence toward the necessarily inhuman glory of battle.]

The dog is the most completely domesticated animal; he is capable even of such human feelings as love and shame. But he is only imperfectly capable; he remains an animal. The dog thus represents man's resistance to acculturation. In Homeric language we would say that the dog lacks *aidōs*. The dog stands for an element within us that is permanently uncivilized. As the dog is a predator within culture, so the dog in us is the predator within us. ⟨...⟩

There is in Homer an instructive contrast between dogs and horses. Both are companions and instruments of man, but they stand to one another rather as Caliban to Ariel. Dogs in Homer are anonymous, but horses have personal names. Horses, like heroes, can have divine parents; they can be immortal; one horse even speaks. Horses thus form a civil series parallel to man; when Hector appeals to his horses ⟨in Book VIII⟩, he does so in terms of reciprocity:

> Xanthus and you, Podargus, Aethon, bright Lampon,
> Now pay me back the care in such abundance
> Andromache gave you, daughter of Eëtion.
> She served you first with grain that honeys the heart
> And mixed you wine to drink when you wanted that,
> Even before me, and I am her husband.
> So come on, bestir yourselves. ⟨. . .⟩

The herdsman has the help of dogs—beasts, like the wild beasts, who can do most of his fighting for him. The warrior has only the help of the peaceful, herbivorous horse. The horse can help him escape from danger, but the warrior must do his own fighting. He must, as it were, be man and dog together—and this, as we have seen is the usual pattern of the similes. ⟨. . .⟩

Combat appears in the similes as a kind of predation in which the enemy appear alternately as competing predators and as prey. The warrior may become (metaphorically) a predator, or he may mobilize the predator (metonymically) within him—that is, the dog. But the dog as metonym shades into the dog as metaphor; in evoking the dog within himself, he runs the risk of becoming a dog, that is, of becoming something less than himself.

This point can be clarified by a further contrast between the dog and the horse. The dog is carnivorous, the horse herbivorous; man is both. Grain, however—the diet of the horse—is not digestible by man until it has been cooked and made into bread. The line between man and horse is fixed by nature. Meat, by contrast, is digestible when raw; it is eaten cooked as a matter of custom. The line between man and dog is fixed only by culture. ⟨. . .⟩

The condition that descends on the warrior in the midst of battle is the *lussa*, a berserk state in which one "respects neither gods nor men." *Lussa* in later Greek means "rabies," and the word has this meaning in Homer also. ⟨. . .⟩

The dog is thus an emblem of the impurity of battle. The warrior becomes a mad dog as he enacts the inner contradiction of battle. On behalf of a human community the warrior is impelled to leave community and act in an inhuman way. He becomes a distorted, impure being; great in his power, he is at the same time reduced to something less than himself. ⟨. . .⟩

On only two heroes does the *lussa* ever descend: on Hector and on Achilles. For Hector the *lussa* is a source of weakness; for Achilles it is a source of strength. Thus these two heroes, driven by fate into a duel, descend together into the pit of impurity—together, but differently. Hector changes from man to dog to meat for dogs; Achilles, from man to devourer of men. Achilles becomes something less than man and at the same time something more; when the fever overtakes him, he becomes a malign demon. Sick himself, he is the bearer of sickness to others. He is both dog and star.

—James M. Redfield, *Nature and Culture in the* Iliad: *The Tragedy of Hector* (Durham: Duke University Press, 1994): pp. 195, 196–97, 201, 202.

JASPER GRIFFIN ON THE GODS AS AUDIENCE

[Jasper Griffin is a professor of Classical Literature at Balliol College, Oxford. His works include *Homer on Life and Death* (1980), *Latin Poets and Roman Life* (1985), and *Virgil* (1986). Below, Griffin examines the gods' role as audience to the events of the *Iliad*. Because they see and pity suffering, and yet—being immortal—have little at stake themselves, the gods are necessarily both more and less significant than the heroes they watch.]

But the gods live at ease and are strangers to death. Consequently they do not possess the heroic qualities which men must learn by accepting destiny, and their 'life of ease' has a sinister side. Three times the phrase appears, and twice the 'gods who live at ease' are described as killing a mortal who has overstepped his limits and trespassed on the divine world. In the *Odyssey*, where the gods are morally on the defensive as they are not in the *Iliad*, and in which Zeus' first words are a justification of the ways of heaven to men, it is notable that the nearest approach to the life of the gods ascribed to any mortals is given to the wicked Suitors,

τούτοισιν μὲν ταῦτα μέλει, κίθαρις καὶ ἀοιδή,
ῥεῖ᾽, ἐπεὶ ἀλλότριον βίοτον νήποινον ἔδουσιν.

'These men care for such things as these, the lyre and singing, at ease, for they devour another's livelihood without paying the price.' Leisure, music, a life of ease, no price: all this is the divine existence presented as an evil. And a cynical view of the joys of heaven seems to underlie the passage where we hear of the throne of Alcinous, 'on which he sits and drinks wine like an immortal.' We seem to be well on the way to that conception of the divine blessedness so elegantly expressed in the Homeric *Hymn to Apollo*: the gods dance as the Muses sing of their own immortal happiness and the misery of men.

Μοῦσαι μέν θ᾽ ἅμα πᾶσαι ἀμειβόμεναι ὀπὶ καλῇ
ὑμνεῦσίν ῥα θεῶν δῶρ᾽ ἄμβροτα ἠδ᾽ ἀνθρώπων
τλημοσύνας, ὅσ᾽ ἔχοντες ὑπ᾽ ἀθανάτοισι θεοῖσι
ζώουσ᾽ ἀφραδέες καὶ ἀμήχανοι, οὐδὲ δύνανται
εὑρέμεναι θανάτοιό τ᾽ ἄκος καὶ γήραος ἄλκαρ.

'The Muses in turn with lovely voices sing of the gods' immortal gifts and the sufferings of men, the things they get at the hands of the immortal gods as they live helpless and defenceless, unable to find a cure for death and a remedy for old age'; and the gods and goddesses dance, and Apollo plays his lyre among them, stepping high, and a shining is all about him; and Zeus and Leto are delighted as they watch their son dancing among the immortal gods. Such a passage, in which divine gaiety has become wholly an end in itself and mortal misery is actually the subject of the singing of the gods (contrast in the *Iliad* I.604), leads to the serenely self-absorbed gods of Epicurus.

In the *Iliad* the blessedness of the gods never quite topples over into mere self-indulgence of this sort. The gods look on and delight in the spectacle, but they are not shown as resembling a bloodthirsty audience at a gladiatorial orgy of carnage, but in a complex light. The idea of the divine watcher of whom justice and indignation are expected is sometimes applied to them, but sometimes they resemble the spectators at a sporting event, and sometimes they are the audience of a tragedy. ⟨...⟩

The gods can always reassert their divinity, show their superiority to men, and retire from the realm of suffering and passion into their blessedness. Now that they no longer have serious wars in heaven, their divine energy might be at a loss without the interest which human history has for them. Their attitude can lead them to suffer, and they watch at times as spectators of a tragedy, rather than a comedy, feeling pity and sorrow, though not of course terror; but their concern cannot rival in intensity that felt by such human watchers as Priam or Achilles. The divine audience both exalts and humbles human action. It is exalted by being made the object of passionate concern to the gods, and at the same time it is shown as trivial in the sublime perspective of heaven.

—Jasper Griffin, *Homer on Life and Death* (Oxford: Oxford University Press, 1980): pp. 191–93, 201.

Oliver Taplin on the Shield of Achilleus

[Oliver Taplin is a Tutorial Fellow at Magdalen College, Oxford, and author of *The Stagecraft of Aeschylus* (1977) and *Comic Angels and Other Approaches to Greek Drama Through Vase-Painting* (1993). Here, he lists other examples of weaponry in Greek literature in order to highlight the oddity of Achilleus' shield, which uniquely depicts images of peace as well as of war. Taplin suggests that Homer uses the Shield to relocate the events of the *Iliad* in the full context of human experience, and so remind his audience of the real cost of Troy.]

Why is the shield of Achilles, instrument of war in a poem of war, covered with scenes of delightful peace, of agriculture, festival, song, and dance? ⟨...⟩

This is the shield that Achilles will carry through the massacre of books 20 and 21 and which will avert Hector's last throw ⟨in Book 22⟩. It is the defiant front presented to the foe by the most terrible killer in the *Iliad*. What would the audience have expected the poet to put on the shield of such a warrior? Consider first the shield which Agamemnon takes up before his gruesome 'aristeia' ⟨in Book 11⟩:

> And he took up the man-enclosing elaborate stark shield,
> a thing of splendour. There were ten circles of bronze upon it,
> and set about it were twenty knobs of tin, pale-shining,
> and in the very centre another knob of dark cobalt.
> And circled in the midst of all was the blank-eyed face of the Gorgon
> with her stare of horror, and Fear was inscribed on it, and Terror.

The demons are designed to inspire terror in the enemy. Compare also the aegis of Zeus donned by Athena (Panic, Strife, and their crew surround the Gorgon's head), and the baldrick which Odysseus sees on the ghost of Heracles ⟨in the *Odyssey*⟩, covered with beasts and carnage. ⟨. . .⟩

So the joys of civilization and fertility on our shield are peculiar. Why all this and not the usual horrors? The question is reinforced by the representations of Achilles' shield in later visual art, which do not try to reproduce Homer's scenes but simply show the Gorgon and other standard devices. More tellingly, Euripides actually protests against the Iliadic shield. The chorus of his *Electra* make it clear that they are singing of the celebrated shield (κλεινᾶς); but it is designed to terrify the Trojans. In the centre it has the sun and constellations, as in Homer, but they are there to panic Hector, and round the edge skims Perseus with the Gorgon's head (a motif from the 'Shield of Heracles'). ⟨. . .⟩

⟨I⟩t might be answered that the shield affords relief from the protracted battle narratives. It is orthodox to claim this as a function of Homeric similes (though most similes are in fact placed to intensify rather than relieve). It is true that the shield takes us far from the Trojan war, but that is hardly enough to explain its detail. After all, the rest of books 18 and 19 are relief from battle scenes. We are still left with the question, why this particular sort of relief? ⟨. . .⟩

⟨O⟩n the whole the scenes are those of prosperous settled societies at peace, representing the Homeric picture of the good life. But the shield is a microcosm, not a utopia, and death and destruction are also there, though in inverse proportion to the rest of the *Iliad*. Rural life is invaded by the lions, and one of the two cities is surrounded by armies and carnage. ⟨ . . . T⟩he city on the shield puts the *Iliad* itself into perspective; it puts war and prowess into perspective within the world as a whole. On the shield the *Iliad* takes up, so to speak, one half of one of the five circles. ⟨...⟩

It is, I suggest, as though there lay behind the *Iliad* the whole world of peace and ordinary life, but only glimpsed occasionally through gaps or windows in the martial canvas which fills the foreground. ⟨...⟩

I trust I do not seem to be maintaining that the *Iliad* is an anti-war epic, a pacifist tract—that would be almost as much of a distortion as the opposite extreme which I am attacking. The *Iliad* does not explicitly condemn war nor does it try to sweeten it: indeed its equity is essential to its greatness. It presents both sides, victory and defeat, the destroyer and the destroyed; and it does not judge between them. The gain and the loss are put side by side without prejudice.

—Oliver Taplin, "The Shield of Achilles Within the Iliad," Greece &
Rome 27, no. 1 (April 1980): pp. 1, 2, 3, 12, 14, 15–16.

RUTH SCODEL ON HOMER'S USE OF MYTH

[Ruth Scodel is a professor of Classical Studies at the University of Michigan, Ann Arbor. Her works include *The Trojan Trilogy of Euripides* (1980) and *Credible Impossibilities: Conventions and Strategies of Verisimilitude in Homer and Greek Tragedy* (1999). In this extract she examines the destruction of the Achaean wall in the *Iliad*, an event that may prefigure the punishment of the Phaiakians in *Odyssey* XIII. Textual irregularities indicate that both episodes are probably descended from Near Eastern myths, which then were imperfectly integrated into poetry.]

The peculiarities of this passage ⟨in Book XII, lines 3–35⟩ have long been noticed. Uniquely, the narrative itself extends beyond the limits of the poem's action in a manner usually confined to prophecies or passages where a character imagines the future. The description seems to contradict the later narrative of 15.361–366, where Apollo levels the wall in the course of battle as easily as a child levels a sandcastle; it is not clear what remains to be destroyed after the war. Poseidon and Apollo destroy the wall by turning the courses of a number of rivers (12.20–25); most of these appear nowhere else in the *Iliad*. ⟨...⟩

The failure to offer hecatombs (mentioned at 7.450 and 12.6) as a reason for the gods' displeasure and the wall's eventual ruin seems like motive-hunting, a commonplace inserted to justify an action with no real cause. Poseidon's worry about his own glory does appear somewhat misplaced: all this fuss over a hastily built wall which does not even succeed in its immediate purpose of protecting the ships is very odd, and if Poseidon or the other gods were truly vexed at the building of the wall, a more active sign of their anger might be expected than the destruction of the wall when the Achaeans no longer have any use for it. ⟨...⟩

The phrase ἡμιθέων γένος ἀνδρῶν ⟨12.23⟩ evokes the Hesiodic depiction of the heroes as a separate race, for γένος in such a context can mean nothing else. In Homer, the continuity of history from the heroes to the poet's contemporaries is complete, although the genre does not call for actual genealogies to link men of the present with those of the past. While the heroes are stronger than later humanity, they are not essentially different. Still, Greek mythology generally falls silent after the Trojan War. The war itself is the richest of Greek myths, and its heroes have extensive traditions, but this rich texture does not outlast their sons. ⟨...⟩

The Trojan War thus functions as a myth of destruction, in which Zeus brings about the catastrophe in order to remove the demigods from the world and separate men from gods. ⟨...⟩ In Near Eastern myth the Deluge has a function like that of the Trojan War in Greek, serving to divide the present age and its world order from an earlier, and in some ways preferable time. ⟨...⟩

The Flood, in which all mankind apart from one survivor and his descendants perish, is a more suitable vehicle for this myth of a prior age. A war, no matter how long and how bitter, does not seem calamitous enough to have been an original form of the myth of destruction; it is, moreover, a normally human and local activity, to be explained historically, rather than a divine visitation. It therefore seems likely that this mythic aspect of the Trojan War is secondary, and that the theme has actually been borrowed from the Deluge. ⟨. . .⟩

⟨T⟩he destruction of the Achaean Wall by a nine-day's rain and the turning of primeval rivers is entirely appropriate. The passage on the wall is unlike any other in the Homeric corpus in its description of the heroes as a γένος of men born of partly divine parentage, and the importance attached to the wall suggests that it stands for something beyond itself: the achievements of its builders. The destruction by flood is not simply a marvelous device. If the motifs which attach themselves to the Trojan War as a myth of destruction are indeed ultimately borrowed from the Near Eastern flood myth, it may not be too surprising that in a single passage the connection of this destruction with water should be maintained. ⟨. . .⟩

The conspicuous use of the theme in connection with the Achaean Wall is thus in some ways typical. The opening of Book 12, like Odysseus' complaint to Agamemnon, breathes a special pathos. The literal flood which wipes away all trace of the Achaean camp preserves its original function; the wall is destroyed less because the poet was afraid of being challenged to point to its remains than because its disappearance gives a solemn air of finality. At its very center, the poem places its events far away in a past which becomes remote and fated not only to end, but to vanish.

—Ruth Scodel, "The Achaean Wall and the Myth of Destruction," *Harvard Studies in Classical Philology* 86 (1982): pp. 33–34, 35, 40, 42–43, 45, 48.

Martin Mueller on the Simile

[Martin Mueller is a professor of English and Classics at Northwestern University, and author of *Children of Oedipus and Other Essays on the Imitation of Greek Tragedy* (1980). In this extract from *The Iliad* (1984), Mueller describes the nature and characteristics of the extended (or "Homeric") simile.]

Out of the more than 300 comparisons in the *Iliad*, close to 200 are of the extended kind. The 'simile with a tail', as Charles Perrault called it in the seventeenth century, has for us become so integral a part of the epic that it is hard to imagine that it may well owe its privileged standing to an idiosyncrasy of the poet of the *Iliad*. ⟨. . .⟩

At the simplest level the simile marks its context as worthy of special attention. Whenever Homer wants to say something important he slows down the pace of the narrative—a procedure that has been much misunderstood. We are all familiar with the term 'epic length', a term which implies that the epic world, unlike the world of drama, is always leisurely and that the urgency of action is subordinated to a stately and imperturbable flow of narrative. The opposite is the case. Homeric narrative has a keen sense of narrative tension and hierarchy, but slowing down is its major tool of emphasis. Its seeming digressions and endless descriptions are, like still shots or slow-motion sequences, moments of heightened suspense. When Pandaros prepares to shoot Menelaos, half a dozen lines are given over to an account of how he made his bow (4.106–11). The description underscores the gravity of the broken truce. The elaborate account of Agamemnon's arming (11.16–45) signals the opening of the Great Battle. The description of Achilles' arms, including 130 lines about his shield, pushes the principle to its extreme. ⟨. . .⟩

It is ⟨. . .⟩ questionable to argue that the major collective function of the similes is to add variety and provide some relief from the grim and monochromatic business of battle. The dominant simile families of hunter–hunted and violent weather are themselves drawn from a very narrow segment of the world and one that is very close to the phenomena of war the similes are meant to illustrate. Rather than provide variety and relief, the dominant simile families underscore the austerity of the poem and intensify its obsession with force and violence. ⟨. . .⟩

What is Iliadic about the *Iliad*? Three points suggest themselves. First, as Paolo Vivante has said, the poet knows 'where to look and what to ignore—how to focus his vision upon the vantage points of reality'. Homer's descriptive mastery is less a matter of technique than of the choice of the image in the first place. ⟨. . .⟩

Second, the image, by virtue of being noticed, is endowed with a significance that does and does not point beyond itself. ⟨. . . T⟩he Iliadic image possesses to an eminent degree the quality many theorists consider the secret of the poetic image: it resists the interpretation it invites. It is not opaque, but it cannot be interpreted away. Whatever thought is inspired by the women at the spring, our gaze never abandons them. The poet creates significance by foregrounding his image—hence the traditional admiration for the plasticity and lucidity of Homeric narrative—and this foregrounding has an arresting power that keeps the reader from abandoning the lively concreteness of the image.

Third, the significant and arresting image is part of a whole of which it is one extreme and which is conveyed in its wholeness as a contrast of polar opposites. This is an example of the pervasive tendency in Greek culture to think of the cosmos, the order of things, as a balance of opposites. The Iliadic totality, however, is unbalanced and moves towards its destruction in one extreme. In the static image of the shield of Achilles war and peace are evenly balanced, but in the narrative war and destruction prevail. Hence the poignancy of such scenes as Hektor's reminiscence of the conversation of boys and girls, the description of the women at the spring, or the flashback to Andromache's wedding: the poet celebrates beauty and order at the point of their destruction.

—Martin Mueller, *The Iliad* (London: George Allen, 1984): pp. 108, 109, 113, 121–22.

Laura M. Slatkin on Thetis

[Laura M. Slatkin is an associate professor of Classical Languages at the University of Chicago and author of *The Power of Thetis: Allusion and Interpretation in the* Iliad (1991). Here she considers the unusual fate of Thetis, whose grief as Achilleus' mother has come about because she was forced to marry a mortal. Had Thetis borne a child to Zeus, it would have overturned the order of the entire cosmos, for her child was fated to be greater than its father; Achilleus' wrath and eventual death thus are intimately linked with the sovereignty of the gods.]

⟨T⟩he *Iliad*'s rendering of Thetis makes hers a grief with a history. ⟨. . .⟩

The primary cause of her suffering was being forced by Zeus, the son of Kronos, to submit against her will to marriage to a mortal. Thus the *Iliad* returns us to the crucial feature of Thetis' mythology, her role in the succession myth. She was forced to marry a mortal because her potential for bearing a son greater than his father meant that marriage to Zeus or Poseidon would begin the entire world order over again. ⟨. . .⟩

If Themis had not intervened, Thetis would have borne to Zeus or Poseidon the son greater than his father, and the entire chain of succession in heaven would have continued: Achilles would have been not the greatest of the heroes, but the ruler of the universe. The price of Zeus' hegemony is Achilles' death. This is the definitive instance of the potency of myths in Homeric epic that exert their influence on the subject matter of the poems yet do not "surface" (using Watkin's term), because of the constraints of the genre. Nevertheless, the poem reveals them, through evocative diction, oblique reference, even conspicuous omission.

It is in this sense that we can understand what appears to be a revision of the prayer formula by Achilles through Thetis to Zeus in Book 1. The typical arrangement of prayers as represented in archaic poetry, we remember, consists of the invocation of the god or goddess, the claim that the person praying is entitled to a favor on the basis of favors granted in the past, and the specific request for a favor in return—based on the premise that this constitutes a formal communication of reciprocal obligations between god and hero.

In directing his request for a favor from Zeus to Thetis, Achilles has translated his reminder of a past favor granted into *her* past aid to Zeus. But he prefaces his request, and invokes his mother, by saying:

μῆτερ, ἐπεί μ' ἔτεκές γε μινυνθάδιόν περ ἐόντα
τιμήν πέρ μοι ὄφελλεν Ολύμπιος ἐγγυαλίξαι
Ζεὺς ὑψιβρεμέτης.

Mother, since you did bear me to be short-lived,
surely high-thundering Olympian Zeus ought to
grant me honor.

In other words, Achilles' favor to Zeus consists in his being *minunthadios*, whereby Zeus's sovereignty is guaranteed. ⟨. . .⟩

The tradition of Thetis's power, the eventual issue of which is in the figure of Achilles, both enhances his stature and is subsumed in it. It thus represents the ultimate example of thematic integration. Heroic epic is concerned with the *erga andrōn* rather than the *erga theōn*. Thus with Achilles the mortal hero, the wrath of Thetis—potent in another framework—becomes absorbed in the actual wrath of her son.

—Laura M. Slatkin, *The Power of Thetis: Allusion and Interpretation in the* Iliad (Berkeley: University of California Press, 1991): pp. 85, 97–98, 101–2, 103.

Thematic Analysis of
the *Odyssey*

The *Odyssey* tells of the adventures of Odysseus, king of Ithaka, whom the sea-god Poseidon prevents from returning home after the Trojan War.

Odysseus' resource is endless: as even Zeus will declare, "There is no mortal half so wise." Like any Homeric hero, he faces an array of dangers, from fabulous storms and monsters to the 108 suitors courting his wife and devouring the substance of his estate. Where the *Iliad* was tragic, however, the *Odyssey* might with some truth be termed a romantic comedy. When Zeus asserts that Aigisthos brought his misfortune upon himself, he is invoking the first of a series of parallels between Odysseus and Agamemnon, whose fates reflect respectively happy and unhappy "endings" to the tale of Troy.

We begin with Odysseus in the middle of his journeys, being detained on Ogygia by the nymph Kalypso. Athene obtains Zeus' permission for the hero's release, and herself goes to visit his son. In the guise of Mentes, she "prophesies" Odysseus' return, advising Telemachos to travel to Pylos and Sparta for news of his whereabouts.

At an assembly the next day [**Book II**], Telemachos attempts to shame the suitors for their behavior. But Antinoös reminds him of the deception of the web, by which Penelope had kept them at bay for three years as she wove through the day—and unwove at night—a shroud for Odysseus' father Laertes. The tale of the web is told twice more in the course of the *Odyssey*, and forms one of its most prominent myths. It is also an early intimation of Penelope's *homophrosynē*, or like-mindedness, with her wily husband Odysseus.

Telemachos learns from Nestor [**Book III**] of the departure from Troy and of Orestes' vengeance upon Aigisthos. In **Book IV** Menelaos reports that Odysseus is alive but held captive by Kalypso.

Our expectation that Telemachos' journey will have a direct relation to Odysseus' own is never fulfilled. Scholars have therefore suggested that the *Odyssey* might better have begun with Odysseus, in **Book V**, but the non-linear "Telemacheia" fulfills a number of key functions in the plot. In the company of the son who never knew him, we are afforded our first glimpses of Odysseus through the eyes of men who did. The homes and homecomings of his fellow-veterans Nestor and Menelaos serve further to heighten the disorder of events at Ithaka. And, too, the analogy with Agamemnon confirms the propriety of Odysseus' revenge: even as Telemachos is expected to show courage (like Orestes), so are the suitors' executions to be regarded as morally justified (like Aigisthos').

Book V returns us to Zeus, who orders Kalypso to release her prisoner. (Since Homer narrates parallel events as though they occur sequentially, this may be understood to happen simultaneously with the events of Book I.) After 17 days at sea, Odysseus comes into sight of Scheria, but Poseidon immediately kindles a storm to prevent his landing. The lament Odysseus here sounds reminds us that death by water, without burial or tribute, is held to be far worse a fate than to have fallen at Troy. Ino spots him and tells him her veil will prevent him from drowning. Characteristically skeptical, Odysseus at first clings to the wreck of his ship, but finally he obeys the nymph and reaches shore.

At Scheria [**Book VI**], Athene visits the king's daughter Nausikaa, inspiring thoughts of marriage so that she will take the royal linens to launder at the seaside. Nausikaa's play with her maids there awakens Odysseus, who asks her guidance to the town. The naked castaway's address to the young girl provides yet another instance of our hero's inventiveness and tact.

King Alkinoös and Queen Arete welcome Odysseus; they offer him assistance and, should he desire it, the princess's hand in marriage. The wanderer thanks them but without hesitation asks to return home. A banquet is ordered in his honor [**Book VIII**], at which the minstrel Demodokos' song of Troy brings tears to Odysseus' eyes. He demonstrates his prowess in a series of athletic contests, which will prefigure his triumph over the suitors at Ithaka. We then hear the song of Hephaistos' trap for his faithless wife Aphrodite and her lover Ares.

Alkinoös calls for gifts for the visitor, which are supplied in plenty. Odysseus next requests a song about the wooden horse, priming his audience—and Homer's—for the dramatic revelation of his name in **Book IX**. There follows the famous account of Odysseus' wanderings, in a flashback that will occupy **Books IX–XII**.

Odysseus' voyages begin with an early pirate raid on the Kikonians, in which the disobedience and folly of his crew are already evident. A storm next drives them to the island of the Lotus Eaters, whose plant robs men of the longing for home. Douglas Frame has posited a connection between the Greek *nóos* ("mind") and *néomai* ("return home"). The episode of the Lotus Eaters may draw on this link, as the *Odyssey* poet binds the qualities of rational intellect and love of home—Odysseus' two dominant characteristics— to so profound an extent that *not* to desire home becomes synonymous with a kind of madness.

The next encounter is with Polyphemos, a Cyclops who devours two of the crew. Odysseus drugs him, and with four of his men drives a heated spike into his eye. Since he has been told his attacker's name is "Nobody," Polyphemos tells others that "Nobody" has hurt him, and no one comes to his aid. But Odysseus, as he leaves, cannot resist a final taunt. The imprudent disclosure of his name enables the Cyclops to call upon his father Poseidon for justice, in a curse that will overshadow the remainder of the hero's journeys.

Odysseus next meets Aiolos, who gives him a bag containing the unfavorable winds. When the crew, suspecting treasure, open the bag, a hurricane is released that blows their ships back to Aiolia.

After losing still more of his crew in a narrow escape from the Laistrygonians, Odysseus comes to Aiaia, where the enchantress Circe turns men into swine. Odysseus subdues her using the herb moly, supplied to him by Hermes. When, after a year's sojourn, the men remind Odysseus to think again of home, Circe instructs him to travel to Hades (Death) to consult Teiresias. Meanwhile Elpenor, the youngest of the crew, falls off a ladder drunk and dies.

In the first *Nekyia*, Odysseus sees the shades of Elpenor, who asks for burial; and of Teiresias, who tells him it is Poseidon who prevents his return. In a warning Circe will echo in Book XII, Teiresias explains that Odysseus and his men can all reach Ithaka, but that if they harm Helios' flocks only Odysseus will survive. Odysseus is also told of a pilgrimage he must eventually make to appease the sea-god. He then meets his mother Antikleia and a number of other figures from legend. At Scheria, Odysseus pauses in his narrative and is congratulated by Alkinoös for telling his tale "as a poet would."

The king asks after the Trojan heroes in Hades, and Odysseus complies with accounts of Agamemnon and Achilleus. Rites are celebrated for Elpenor, and Circe warns Odysseus against the Sirens, the monster Skylla, and the whirlpool Charybdis.

The Sirens' song makes Odysseus long to turn the ship. But the crew, whose ears have been sealed with beeswax, remain deaf to his entreaties and sail safely past. Skylla, however, seizes and devours six of the men, an event Odysseus will later recall as the worst he would ever have to endure.

At Thrinakia, Odysseus wants to sail on, but Eurylochos convinces the tired crew to stop. When the starving men slaughter his cattle, Zeus answers Helios' demand for restitution by destroying their ships. Odysseus, the lone survivor, manages to save himself from Charybdis by clinging "like a bat" to a fig tree. His landing on Ogygia finally closes the circle, returning us to the account he has already given to Alkinoös and Arete in Book VII.

The Phaiakians, who are magical sailors, take Odysseus home [**Book XIII**], leaving him asleep on the beach at Ithaka. On the way back, Zeus allows the still-vengeful Poseidon to turn their ship into stone.

On waking, Odysseus thinks the Phaiakians have tricked him, but Athene, appearing as a shepherd, convinces him he has arrived at Ithaka. The wanderer quickly invents a false account of himself in the first of the "Cretan narratives," to which the goddess responds with delight: "Two of a kind, we are, / contrivers, both." Disguising him as an old beggar, she sends him to the hut of the swineherd Eumaios [**Book XIV**], who welcomes Odysseus and treats him hospitably.

Athene next visits Telemachos in Lakedaimon [**Book XV**] to urge him home. Helen interprets the flight of a mountain eagle as a portent of Odysseus' revenge, and the fugitive Theoklymenos reads a second omen signifying that the royal family "will be in power forever" at Ithaka.

Instructed by Athene, Odysseus reveals his identity to his son [**Book XVI**]. At the palace Telemachos relates his travels to Penelope [**Book XVII**], and Theoklymenos announces that the king has already returned. However, only his old, dying dog Argos recognizes the beggar as Odysseus himself. When Antinoös hurls a footstool at him, a suitor warns that gods are wont to travel disguised as beggars. But Antinoös shrugs this off, adding impiety to his other crimes.

The tramp Iros quarrels with Odysseus [**Book XVIII**], who thrashes him and puts him outside. Odysseus next warns Amphinomos, who has spoken to him kindly, of "Odysseus'" impending return, but Athene strips the suitor of his resolve to go. Penelope then reappears, so beautified by Athene that the suitors all swear again to have her. Her cunning in extracting gifts from them gladdens the heart of the watching Odysseus.

Questioned by Penelope [**Book XIX**], the "beggar" responds with another of the Cretan tales, claiming to have met the king and describing his clothing minutely. He gives a largely true account of the events at Thrinakia and Scheria, and swears that Odysseus will return "before the crescent moon." Penelope professes disbelief but summons the nurse Eurykleia, who recognizes Odysseus by a scar on his leg. The narrative is then suspended for a digression of nearly 200 lines, as we learn the history of the wound, which was inflicted during a boar-hunt in Odysseus' youth. We also are told the origins of his name, which means both "much suffering" and "much suffered," which was bestowed by Odysseus' grandfather Autolykos.

In her joy, Eurykleia nearly reveals the stranger's identity, but Odysseus quickly seizes her and commands silence. Penelope, coming out of her reverie, tells a dream of the impending vengeance and gives the famous account of the gates of horn and ivory through which all dreams, false or true, must pass. She further describes the test she will set the next day, and her intention of marrying whoever can string Odysseus' bow and shoot an arrow through a line of 12 axe-heads. Odysseus assures her that her husband will by then have returned. (Philip Whaley Harsh and Robert Fitzgerald, among others, have suggested that Penelope is by now aware of the stranger's identity.)

In **Book XX,** Athene instills a turn of hysteria in the suitors, lending a phantasmagoric quality to the scene. Penelope then brings Odysseus' bow from the storeroom [**Book XXI**], and Odysseus takes the loyal cowherd (Philoitios) and swineherd (Eumaios) into his confidence. When nearly all of the suitors have failed at stringing the bow, the still-disguised "beggar" asks to be allowed an attempt. Penelope overrides the suitors' objections, but Telemachos sends her back to her loom, ordering that the contest be left to him. Odysseus then strings the bow: "the taut gut vibrating hummed and sang / a swallow's note." (A swallow was the bird traditionally associated with return.) At a thunderclap from Zeus, Odysseus aims and shoots. The arrow passes easily through all 12 axe-heads.

A bloodbath follows [**Book XXII**], with Odysseus sending a second arrow through Antinoös' throat. With Athene deflecting most of the enemy fire, Odysseus, Telemachos, Philoitios, and Eumaios dispatch all of the men, sparing only the minstrel Phemios and the herald Medon. Eurykleia, on seeing the dead suitors, is about to raise a cry of triumph but is stopped by Odysseus. The 12 maids who have had illicit affairs with the suitors are made to remove the bodies and clean the hall, and then—in one of the epic's most brutal moments—they are summarily hanged.

After purifying the hall with sulfur, Odysseus sends for Penelope [**Book XXIII**]. The queen, still wary of impostors, alludes to tokens of recognition only she and the real Odysseus can know. He agrees to the test and is roused to anger only when Penelope tells him his bed has been moved. We find then that the couple's bed—and their home—was built around the fixed trunk of an olive tree; this is the ultimate sign, and Penelope acknowledges her husband at last.

In Book V, the drowning Odysseus' first sight of land was compared to a father's reunion with his family; his reunion with Penelope now is compared to a drowning swimmer's first sight of land. The themes of reunion, of homecoming, and of danger at sea are thus all returned to a single point.

Agamemnon himself makes the epic's final reference to the Oresteia-cycle when he praises Penelope for her faithfulness in the second *Nekyia* [**Book XXIV**]. Meanwhile Odysseus, on finding Laertes in his orchard, continues to dissemble, perhaps out of habit. Perceiving the old man's suffering, however, he finally admits his identity.

News of Odysseus' revenge has spread, and the suitors' families come seeking vengeance. At the warnings of Medon and Halitherses, most give up their quarrel; the rest pursue Odysseus, led by Antinoös' father. Telemachos, now grown up, assures Odysseus he is ready for any further test; and Laertes, rejoicing at his son's and grandson's valor, strikes Eupeithes down himself. But Athene prevents full-scale fighting, and the epic draws to a close as peace is made at Ithaka.

Modern readers often find themselves more in sympathy with Odysseus' plight than with Achilleus' or Hektor's. James Joyce caught at least part of the reason for this in his famous remark that Odysseus is "complete": the heroes of the *Iliad*, for all their towering sublimity, manifestly are not. There is, too, something universal, even archetypal, for us in the hero pitted against a sea of troubles—the travails of life—with only Athene, or Wisdom, to guide him.

But the epic's persistent popularity may be even simpler than that. "The purpose of Odysseus," Fitzgerald observed wryly, "is to get home and to prevail there." And this may well be the best tribute to be made to the *Odyssey*—the poem that has dreamed, for nearly three thousand years, of what it might mean for any of us to get home and to prevail there. ❀

Critical Views on
the *Odyssey*

SAMUEL BUTLER ON THE AUTHORITY OF WOMEN

[The works of Samuel Butler (1835–1902) include *Erewhon* (1872) and *The Way of All Flesh* (1903), as well as prose translations of the *Iliad* and *Odyssey*. Butler believed that the *Odyssey* poet was a woman, probably young and almost certainly unmarried. In *The Authoress of the Odyssey* (1897), he presents evidence for the superior strength and influence of the poem's women over its men.]

Who are the women in the "Odyssey"? There is Minerva, omnipresent at the elbows of Ulysses and Telemachus to keep them straight and alternately scold and flatter them. In the "Iliad" she is a great warrior but she is no woman: in the "Odyssey" she is a great woman but no warrior; we have, of course, Penelope—masterful nearly to the last and tossed off to the wings almost from the moment that she has ceased to be so; Euryclea, the old servant, is quite a match for Telemachus, "do not find fault, child," she says to him, "when there is no one to find fault with." Who can doubt that Helen is master in the house of Menelaus—of whom all she can say in praise is that he is "not deficient either in person or understanding"? Idothea in Book IV. treats Menelaus *de haut en bas*, all through the Proteus episode. She is good to him and his men, but they must do exactly what she tells them, and she evidently enjoys "running" them—for I can think of no apter word. Calypso is the master mind, not Ulysses. ⟨. . .⟩

Take Nausicaa again, delightful as she is, it would not be wise to contradict her; she knows what is good for Ulysses, and all will go well with him so long as he obeys her, but she must be master and he man. I see I have passed over Ino in Book V. She is Idothea over again, just as Circe is Calypso, with very little variation. Who again is master—Queen Arēte or King Alcinous? Nausicaa knows well enough how to answer this question. When giving her instructions to Ulysses she says:—

> "Never mind my father, but go up to my mother and embrace her knees; if she is well disposed towards you there is some chance of your getting home to see your friends again." ⟨. . .⟩

The moral in every case seems to be that man knows very little, and cannot be trusted not to make a fool of himself even about the little that he does know, unless he has a woman at hand to tell him what he ought to do. There is not a single case in which a man comes to the rescue of female beauty in distress; it is invariably the other way about.

The only males who give Ulysses any help while he is on his wanderings are Æolus, who does him no real service and refuses to help him a second time, and Mercury, who gives him the herb Moly (x. 305) to protect him against the spells of Circe. In this last case, however, I do not doubt that the writer was tempted by the lovely passage ⟨in the *Iliad,* Book XXIV⟩ where Mercury meets Priam to conduct him to the Achæan camp; one pretty line, indeed (and rather more), of the Iliadic passage above referred to is taken bodily by the writer of the "Odyssey" to describe the youth and beauty of the god. With these exceptions, throughout the poem Andromeda rescues Perseus, not Perseus Andromeda—Christiana is guide and guardian to Mr. Greatheart, not Mr. Greatheart to Christiana. ⟨. . .⟩

A woman if she attempts an Epic is almost compelled to have a man for her central figure, but she will minimise him, and will maximise his wife and daughters, drawing them with subtler hand. That the writer of the "Odyssey" has done this is obvious; and this fact alone should make us incline strongly towards thinking that we are in the hands not of a man but of a woman.

—Samuel Butler, *The Authoress of the Odyssey* (Chicago: University of Chicago Press, 1967): pp. 107, 108, 109, 114.

ERICH AUERBACH ON HOMER'S PERSPECTIVE

[Erich Auerbach was Professor of Comparative Literature at Yale University. His works include *Mimesis: The Representation of Reality in Western Literature* (1946), *Dante: Poet of the Secular World* (1961), and *Literary Language and Its Public in Late Latin Antiquity and in the Middle Ages* (1965). This extract from his celebrated essay on "Odysseus' Scar" considers the function of digressions in Homer.

⟨T⟩he element of suspense is very slight in the Homeric poems; nothing in their entire style is calculated to keep the reader or hearer breathless. The digressions are not meant to keep the reader in suspense, but rather to relax the tension. ⟨. . .⟩

The "retarding element," the "going back and forth" by means of episodes, seems to me, too, in the Homeric poems, to be opposed to any tensional and suspensive striving toward a goal, and doubtless Schiller is right in regard to Homer when he says that what he gives us is "simply the quiet existence and operation of things in accordance with their natures"; Homer's goal is "already present in every point of his progress." ⟨. . .⟩ The true cause of the impression of "retardation" appears to me to lie elsewhere—namely, in the need of the Homeric style to leave nothing which it mentions half in darkness and unexternalized. ⟨. . .⟩

One might think that the many interpolations, the frequent moving back and forth, would create a sort of perspective in time and place; but the Homeric style never gives any such impression. The way in which any impression of perspective is avoided can be clearly observed in the procedure for introducing episodes, a syntactical construction with which every reader of Homer is familiar; it is used in the passage we are considering, but can also be found in cases when the episodes are much shorter. To the word scar (v. 393) there is first attached a relative clause ("which once long ago a boar . . ."), which enlarges into a voluminous syntactical parenthesis; into this an independent sentence unexpectedly intrudes (v. 396: "A god himself gave him . . ."), which quietly disentangles itself from syntactical subordination, until, with verse 399, an equally free syntactical treatment of the new content begins a new present which continues unchallenged until, with verse 467 ("The old woman now touched it . . ."), the scene which had been broken off is resumed. To be sure, in the case of such long episodes as the one we are considering, a purely syntactical connection with the principal theme would hardly have been possible; but a connection with it through perspective would have been all the easier had the content been arranged with that end in view; if, that is, the entire story of the scar had been presented as a recollection which awakens in Odysseus' mind at this particular moment. It would have been perfectly easy to do; the story of the scar had only to be inserted two verses earlier, at the first mention of the word scar, where the motifs "Odysseus" and "recollection" were already at hand. But any such subjectivistic-perspectivistic procedure, creating a foreground and background, resulting in the present lying open to the depths of the past, is entirely foreign to the Homeric style; the Homeric style knows only a foreground, only a uniformly illuminated, uniformly objective present. And so the excursus does not begin until two lines later, when Euryclea has discovered the scar—the possibility for a perspectivistic connection no longer exists, and the story of the wound becomes an independent and exclusive present. ⟨. . .⟩

The oft-repeated reproach that Homer is a liar takes nothing from his effectiveness, he does not need to base his story on historical reality, his reality is powerful enough in itself; it ensnares us, weaving its web around us, and that suffices him. And the "real" world into which we are lured, exists for itself, contains nothing but itself; the Homeric poems conceal nothing, they contain no teaching and no secret second meaning. Homer can be analyzed, ⟨. . .⟩ but he cannot be interpreted.

—Erich Auerbach, *Mimesis: The Representation of Reality in Western Literature*, Willard R. Trask, trans. (Berne: A. Francke, 1946): pp. 4, 5, 7, 13.

W. B. STANFORD ON THE AMBIGUITY OF THE ODYSSEUS FIGURE

[W. B. Stanford taught at Trinity College, Dublin; his books include *Greek Metaphor: Studies in Theory and Practice* (1936) and *The Enemies of Poetry* (1980). In this extract from *The Ulysses Theme* (1954), he describes how and why the figure of Homer's Odysseus has been refracted into more specialized types in later literature, sometimes appealing (as in *Ulysses*) and sometimes not (as in the *Philoktetes*).]

One other aspect of Odysseus' Homeric character needs to be kept in mind at the last. In a way it is the most important of all for the development of the tradition. This is the fundamental ambiguity of his essential qualities. We have seen how prudence may decline towards timidity, tactfulness towards a blameworthy *suppressio veri*, serviceability towards servility, and so on. The ambiguity lies both in the qualities themselves and in the attitudes of others towards them. Throughout the later tradition this ambiguity in Odysseus's nature and in his reputation will vacillate between good and bad, between credit and infamy. Odysseus's personality and reputation at best are poised, as it were, on a narrow edge between Aristotelian faults of excess and deficiency. Poised between rashness and timorousness, he is prudently brave; poised between rudeness and obsequiousness he is 'civilized'; poised between stupidity and over-cleverness he, at his best, is wise.

Homer was large-minded enough to comprehend a unity in apparent diversity, a structural consistency within an external changefulness, in the character of Ulysses. But few later authors were as comprehending. Instead, in the post-Homeric tradition, Odysseus's complex personality becomes broken up into various simple types—the *politique*, the romantic amorist, the sophisticated villain, the sensualist, the philosophic traveller, and others. Not till James Joyce wrote his *Ulysses* was a successful effort made to recreate Homer's polytropic hero in full. Similarly after Homer judgments on Odysseus's ethical status become narrower and sharper. Moralists grew angry in disputing whether he was a 'good' man or not—good, that is to say, according to the varying principles of Athens, or Alexandria, or Rome, or Florence, or Versailles, or Madrid, or Weimar. Here is another long Odyssey for Odysseus to endure. But Homer, the unmoved mover in this chaotic cosmos of tradition, does not vex his own or his hero's mind with any such problems in split personality or ambivalent ethics. He is content to portray a man of many turns.

—W. B. Stanford, *The Ulysses Theme: A Study in the Adaptability of a Traditional Hero* (Oxford: Basil Blackwell, 1954): pp. 79–80.

[William S. Anderson taught at Yale University. This extract from his essay on "Calypso and Elysium" (1958) compares Kalypso's isle of Ogygia, on which Odysseus is offered immortality and a life of ease, with the Elysian paradise Menelaos is promised in the afterlife. Drawing upon the unhappiness of Menelaos' current existence, and the strong associations both islands have with death, Anderson shows how Odysseus could have rejected an apparently ideal life.]

Menelaus has surrounded himself with all the physical comforts which wealth can buy, and, although he is in all likelihood the richest man in the world, he has not found happiness in these glittering halls. He has lived with Zeus' daughter for ten years since the destruction of Troy, and still both have little in common and easily yield to their divergent memories of the past. If any man can be said to rival the gods, as Telemachus innocently remarks, Menelaus is that man, with his Olympian wealth and his wife like Artemis. In character, then, Elysium offers him no compensation for earthly trials; rather, it continues the same sensuous tenor of his present existence. ⟨...⟩

On Calypso's Isle, the poet presents Odysseus overcoming temptations which define his attitude not only towards home, but, even more important, towards life itself. The significance of the hero's action becomes especially clear, I hope to show, because Homer has carefully placed Odysseus in the very environment which has been promised to Menelaus. ⟨...⟩

The climates of the two islands assume considerable importance in Homer's description, for they bear directly upon the significance of the places to their residents, Menelaus or Odysseus. The balmy wind, the freedom from seasonal variation, in contrast of course with the climate which the Greeks experienced, convey the data necessary to support Homer's assertion, that life in Elysium is supremely easy. Such a life, as the fact that Menelaus has earned it through marriage with Zeus' daughter suggests, approximates divine felicity. The same freedom from seasonal changes Homer attributes to the gods' residence. Ogygia, too, proves so congenial to divine senses that, on his arrival there, Hermes pauses in admiration. The scene which has evoked Hermes' admiration possesses all the qualities of the island paradise: Ogygia has luxuriant growth of trees and vines, swarms with birds, abounds in water; and colorful flowers dot nearby meadows. All centers on the cave of Calypso, from which emerge the seductive notes of the nymph's song and the pleasant scent of burning cedar logs. This idyllic description implies the same gentle regularity of climate as on Elysium, the same effortlessness of existence. Like Elysium, therefore, Ogygia can confer upon Odysseus immortality, with all that the term connotes of security and sensuous ease. ⟨. . .⟩

⟨B⟩oth Elysium and Ogygia possess important associations with death. According to the prophecy of Proteus, Menelaus will escape death in Argos and be transported to the felicity of Elysium, from which we can infer that Elysium represents the desire for and possibility of personal survival after death. Because of his connection with the semi-divine Helen, Menelaus himself attains a divine state of existence, escaping the fate allotted to humanity as a whole. We have already discussed the impression which such felicity makes against the background of Sparta. In the case of Calypso's Isle, the immortality offered to Odysseus contains many suggestions not of eternal life, but of eternal death. ⟨. . .⟩ Güntert takes the traditional etymology of Calypso's name, the "Concealer," and, because of Homer's usage of the verb *kalúptein*, specifically interprets Calypso as "she who buries." He interprets the name Ogygia as referring to the Underworld, Stygian. The trees and flowers surrounding the cave of the nymph, conceivable as an entrance to Hades, connote death. The black alder (*klé•thre•*) is probably funereal; the black poplar (*aígeiros*) Homer describes as growing also in Hades, in the glades of Persephone; and the cypress still marks the location of cemeteries in Italy and Greece. The flowery meadows, parallel to the fields of asphodel through which Achilles strides, display parsley and the purple iris, both associated with the funeral ritual. ⟨. . .⟩

While Menelaus looks bitterly to the past or wearily to his Elysian escape from life, Odysseus emerges from the past a new man, entirely committed to living values. His greatness depends utterly on his humanity, his mortality. The Greeks understood clearly Odysseus' rejection of Calypso, and tradition has respected him by never assigning him to Elysium.

—William S. Anderson, "Calypso and Elysium," *Classical Journal* 54, no. 1 (October 1958): pp. 5, 6–7, 10.

[Cedric H. Whitman was Eliot Professor of Greek at Harvard University. His works include *Sophocles: A Study of Heroic Humanism* (1951), *Aristophanes and the Comic Hero* (1964), and *Heroic Paradox* (1982). In this extract from *Homer and the Heroic Tradition* (1958), he examines the styles of Geometric and proto-Attic vase-painting as they mirror the descriptive methods of the *Iliad* and *Odyssey*, respectively.]

It can hardly be entirely fanciful to see in the change from the Geometric to the proto-Attic approach an analogy to the shift of outlook from the *Iliad* to the *Odyssey*. This is no mere matter of subject. It involves the whole instinct about the inner relationship of part to whole, of decoration to structure, as well as the basic conception of humanity and its context. The triumph of scenic episode over totality of design is perhaps the most striking parallel between the *Odyssey* and proto-Attic art. Yet the parallel extends also to many details of the creative approach. In the *Iliad*, battle scenes contain many summaries of unknown men slain by unknown men, *androktasiae;* these anonymities are, however, always named, and their little entries, as in the *Catalogue*, pass by with formulaic rigidity, like the rows of identical warriors on Geometric ware. Individuals become visible only through the shape of a norm. But in the *Odyssey*, the companions of Odysseus are treated differently. They fall into no formalized pattern of the whole, and only one or two are named at all. For the most part, they disappear until they have to do something, and are treated, in contrast to the brief tragic histories of the *Iliad*, as simple expendabilities. Proto-Attic art is not concerned to represent generalities of men, but particularities of event; and hence, instead of the typical scene, formulaic yet possibly individualized to a faint degree, there is either full individualization or nothing. Two of the companions emerge as people, the young, heedless and ill-fated Elpenor, and the presumptuous, sane, and slightly insubordinate Eurylochus. The rest are vapor. It is often said that the characters in the *Odyssey* are types, and some are. But they are regularly types of something in human experience, and never, with the exception of Odysseus himself, typical simply of humanity, as are the rows of names in the *Iliad*. No such generality runs through the *Odyssey*: its pictures seize the foreground and thrust out the binding continuous friezes.

Moreover, in the matter of characterization the methods of the *Iliad* and *Odyssey* differ. As described elsewhere, the secondary characters of the *Iliad* find their individuality through a series of subtle contrasts, either with the heroic norm, or with another character, usually Achilles. Personal details, especially of a trivial sort, play little or no part. But the *Odyssey* is directly descriptive, as a rule through illustrative action, sometimes even in minor detail. We learn the character of Eumaeus from his defense of the stranger from the dogs, from his manner of putting food before a guest, from his tears at the sight of Telemachus, from his strict obedience to orders, from his sedulous care of the swine, and a hundred other touches. Here is no characterization by reference to a single formulaic social norm. The poet is interested both in Eumaeus and in his total context; he wants to fill him out. ⟨. . .⟩ So too of the details of personal appearance, one hears little or nothing in the *Iliad*, but in the *Odyssey* the hero's dark hair and stout limbs are often mentioned, especially in connection with his transformation by Athena. In particular, skin quality has newly impressed itself on the poet's imagination: Odysseus is darkly tanned, Penelope's skin is like cut ivory. Such minutiae are unknown to the Geometric *Iliad*, though women in general are "white-armed"; but in the proto-Attic period, the vase-painters were beginning to represent flesh tones with different colors, white as a rule, but sometimes black for men, and it is perhaps no wonder that this new pictorial element has crept into the epic consciousness. Finally, in the matter of landscape and milieu, it is hard to find any descriptive passages in the *Iliad* comparable to that of the island of Calypso or the gardens of Alcinous. Here simple delight in the setting has tempted the poet to sing on and on, regardless of symmetry or waiting issues. New fields of content have revealed themselves, and the older concept of form has become attenuated amid the new preoccupation with the immediacy of life.

—Cedric H. Whitman, *Homer and the Heroic Tradition* (Cambridge, Mass.: Harvard University Press, 1958): pp. 291–92, 293.

ANNE AMORY ON THE PSYCHOLOGY OF ODYSSEUS AND PENELOPE

[Anne Amory was a lecturer in Classics at Yale University and the author of *Blameless Aegisthus: A Study of AMYMΩN and Other Homeric Epithets* (1973). Her essay on "The Gates of Horn and Ivory" (1966) offers a detailed analysis of the Gates of Dreams Penelope describes to the disguised Odysseus in Book XIX. Here Amory shows (transparent) horn to represent the predominantly rational Odysseus, whereas (opaque) ivory tends more to be associated with Penelope, whose perceptions are intuitive.]

The third interpretation from Eustathius has suffered a curious neglect, perhaps because it seems too simple:

> Some say that the true [gate] is of horn, that is, transparent,
> whereas the false [gate] is of ivory, that is, blurred or opaque,
> because it is possible to see through horn . . . but not through ivory.

This explanation, as we shall see eventually, comes the closest to what I think Homer intended in the speech he gave Penelope. ⟨. . .⟩

⟨I⟩t seems to me that the passage about the gates of dreams has exercised a sort of magnetic effect on the surrounding decorative passages, and that these are phrased in such a way and so placed as to complement and clarify the meaning of the dreams passage. The result is that in the *Odyssey* horn is associated with plainly recognizable truth and with Odysseus, while ivory is associated with deceptive truth and with Penelope. ⟨. . .⟩

The passage about the key brings ivory and horn together, for beyond the simple fact that the key opens the storeroom in which the bow is kept, the descriptions of Penelope using the key and Odysseus the bow are curiously similar. Penelope shoots back the bolts, aiming straight in front, and the doors let forth a sound like the roar of a bull:

> ἐν δὲ κληῖδ᾽ ἧκε, θυρέων δ᾽ ἀνέκοπτεν ὀχῆας
> ἄντα τιτυσκομένη· τὰ δ᾽ ἀνέβραχεν ἠΰτε ταῦρος
> βοσκόμενος λειμῶνι.

When Odysseus tries the string of the bow, it sings like a swallow under his touch:

δεξιτερῇ δ᾽ ἄρα χειρὶ λαβὼν πειρήσατο νευρῆς·
ἡ δ᾽ ὑπὸ καλὸν ἄεισε, χελιδόνι εἰκέλη αὐδήν.

Then he shoots an arrow straight through the axes, aiming right in front:

αὐτόθεν ἐκ δίφροιο καθήμενος, ἧκε δ᾽ ὀϊστὸν
ἄντα τιτυσκόμενος, πελέκεων δ᾽ οὐκ ἤμβροτε πάντων.

One critic has seen in this parallel an instinctive use of sexual symbolism, but even if we reject this comment as fanciful, it is true that the passages put Odysseus and Penelope into a similar situation, with the crucial difference that horn is connected with Odysseus, who knows the complete truth, while ivory is associated with Penelope who does not. For Penelope, in getting the bow and announcing the contests, acts on the inspiration of Athena (21.1–2), without being fully aware of the true situation. ⟨. . .⟩

Odysseus and Penelope, in spite of their similarities, and in spite of the ὁμοφροσύνη between them, look at the world in very different ways. Odysseus observes most things unwaveringly, as he does Penelope's tears in 19, for example; and what he sees is immediately recognized by him as real. ⟨. . .⟩

Penelope is passive and intuitive. She looks at things only intermittently; she is always holding a veil in front of her face, or looking away from things. She does not notice Telemachus' absence at the beginning of the poem, nor does she observe Eurycleia's recognition of the beggar (19.478). When she finally comes to Odysseus after the suitors are dead, she cannot look directly into his face (23.106–7). What she does see is not exactly false, but it is often mysterious, and its truth is not, and cannot be, instantly apparent. Moreover, she tends to deny or deprecate the truth of what she really does see and feel. Yet her perceptions are ultimately accurate, and the actions which she undertakes on the basis of her half-glimpsed, intuitive, tentatively acknowledged feelings always turn out to be exactly the right ones.

—Anne Amory, "The Gates of Horn and Ivory," *Yale Classical Studies* 20 (1966): pp. 6, 50–51, 53–54, 55–56.

[Sir Hugh Lloyd-Jones is Emeritus Professor of Greek at Christ Church, Oxford, and author of *Blood for the Ghosts* (1982) and *Greek in a Cold Climate* (1991). In this extract from *The Justice of Zeus* (1971) he shows the moral viewpoint of the *Odyssey* to be more simplistic than that of the *Iliad*, and attributes this to the respective genres of the two poems.]

Soon after the opening of the poem, Zeus in the assembly of the gods comments on the death of Aegisthus, the murderer of Agamemnon, at the hands of his victim's son Orestes. Mortals, he complains, blame the gods for sending them evil, but in truth they themselves through their wicked recklessness have to endure pains beyond what is fated. When Aegisthus was plotting to make love to Agamemnon's wife and kill her husband, the gods even sent their messenger Hermes to warn him of the inevitable consequences, but Aegisthus rejected the warning and has now paid the penalty. This speech of Zeus implies a belief radically different from that found in the *Iliad*. There the god puts evil ideas, no less that good ideas, into men's minds; that is how men's *moira*, the portion assigned them by the gods, comes to be fulfilled. When the god wishes to destroy a man, he sends Ate to take away his wits. But now Zeus denies that the gods put evil ideas into the minds of men, and even claims that they warn men against the evil ideas they themselves have thought of.

"Placed where it is, at the very beginning of the poem," says Dodds, "the remark sounds . . . programmatic": and in the *Odyssey* as a whole the programme which it announces is carried out. In the first half of the poem, the companions of Odysseus are warned by Tiresias of what will happen if they slaughter the cattle of the Sun; in the second half, the suitors are warned first by the old man Halitherses and later by the prophet Theoclymenus of what will happen if they persist in their wooing of Penelope. Gods often put good or clever ideas into the minds of men; Athene, for example, is constantly inspiring Odysseus with such notions; but evil ideas the gods never inspire. ⟨. . .⟩

Achilles and Hector, Helen and Agamemnon are not easily to be classified as good or bad; the issues between Greeks and Trojans, between Achilles and Agamemnon are not (despite the considerations regarding justice) easily to be seen as conflicts between black and white. In the *Odyssey*, moral issues are infinitely simpler; not only during the adventures narrated by Odysseus, with their marked element of folktale, but even in Ithaca, where daily life is depicted with such great naturalism, good and bad and right and wrong are separated almost as clearly as in a Western film. True, one or two characters have an intermediate status; there are the suitor Amphinomus, to whom Odysseus gives good advice that is not taken, and Phemius and Medon, who keep company with the suitors against their will; but these exceptions hardly do more than heighten the contrast between black and white. It seems most unsafe to conclude that the comparative moral simplicity of the *Odyssey* is due simply to ethical progress made by the Greek world in the interval between the composition of the two poems. The truth is that the *Odyssey* is not an epic poem of the same kind as the *Iliad*. It is a poem linked with the true heroic epic through the person of its hero and other characters, yet containing a strong element of folklore and distinguished by a marked moralising strain, conducive to the triumph of the hero, and a happy ending, from the tragic character of the other epic.

—Hugh Lloyd-Jones, *The Justice of Zeus* (Berkeley: University of California Press, 1971): pp. 28–29, 31.

BERNARD FENIK ON ZEUS' JUSTICE AND POSEIDON'S REVENGE

[Bernard Fenik is the author of *Iliad X and the Rhesus* (1964) and *Homer and the Nibelungenlied* (1986). In this extract from *Studies in the* Odyssey (1974), he contrasts the morality Zeus seems to prescribe at the opening of the *Odyssey* with the purely vengeful behavior of Poseidon and, later, Helios. Unlike Lloyd-Jones, Fenik believes the poet to be more concerned with a coherent style than with a coherent ethics.]

Aigisthus slew Agamemnon in pre-meditated murder and then married his victim's widow, both deeds in defiance of the gods' express admonitions that Orestes would be sure to exact revenge. Evil intent, warning from on high, persistence in criminal action, deserved retribution—the suitors, whose fate the story of Aigisthus is meant to illuminate and predict, follow an identical course into the same ruin. ⟨. . .⟩ The gods' concern for human behavior, and the ethical categories which the story of the hero's return will exemplify, and in terms of which the suitors' catastrophe is to be judged, are thus established right from the start. The fate of Odysseus' crew is explained in the same terms: like Aigisthus (and therefore like the suitors) they perished because of their own ἀτασθαλίαι—reckless folly—and accordingly lost their chance to make it home. ⟨. . .⟩

But when we consider how Odysseus incurs the wrath of Poseidon, it becomes immediately clear that the same motif of wise advice disregarded conceals a profound difference in the circumstances and acts that call forth the punishment. ⟨. . . T⟩he blinding was justified in terms of Homeric or any other morality: Odysseus and his men would have perished if they had not acted, and the hero's furious boasting does not turn the deed from self-defense into wanton criminality. Odysseus makes a bad mistake, a tactical error, but he does not commit a "sin". ⟨. . .⟩

⟨I⟩t is impossible to justify Odysseus' suffering at the hands of Poseidon in terms of Zeus' explanation of guilt and punishment in the prologue, or to catalogue Odysseus along with Aigisthus and the suitors as another example of how man brings his own troubles upon him. Zeus was clearly thinking of men of a genuine and consistent criminal temper, not of somebody like Odysseus who suffers for a momentary and understandable aberration. We are forced to conclude that the ethical standards set forth by Zeus do not apply to the Poseidon-Odysseus story, or to put it another way, that the religious and moral outlook of the Odyssey is not uniform. ⟨. . .⟩

Helios' anger, like Poseidon's, focuses upon a factual guilt consequent upon a single act: the crew *did* eat the sacred cattle, just as Odysseus *did* blind Polyphemos. But the men are actually driven to the act by the very gods who punish them for it. ⟨. . .⟩

I conclude that neither the anger of Helios nor of Poseidon conforms to Zeus' excursus in the prologue, but that together they form a pair in their divine character, as they do in the external similarities of narration. ⟨. . .⟩

The epics represent a historical, cultural, linguistic and intellectual amalgam. They are a rich storehouse of contributions from many epochs and generations of poets. Their unity does not consist of a logically conceived philosophical or theological system, in which everything in this world is integrated into a neatly distributed whole. Unity consists rather in certain narrative structures and in dominant emphases imposed upon a complex substructure. The angers of Helios and Poseidon do indeed contradict Zeus' words in the prologue. But they are so similar to each other both in general and in so many particulars as to belong unmistakably to the whole larger class of doublets in the Odyssey. They contribute to the stylistic unity of the epic as much as they disturb its ethical uniformity. The story is always the same: strong stylistic tendencies and narrative emphases take precedence over a consistent world-outlook.

—Bernard Fenik, *Studies in the Odyssey* (Wiesbaden: Franz Steiner Verlag, 1974): pp. 210, 211, 213, 215, 219.

NORMAN AUSTIN ON LANDSCAPES OF ORDER AND DISORDER

[Norman Austin is a professor of Classics at the University of Arizona. His books include *Meaning and Being in Myth* (1990) and *Helen of Troy and Her Shameless Phantom* (1994). This extract from *Archery at the Dark of the Moon* (1975) examines the ecology and architecture of the worlds Odysseus encounters on his travels. The narrative's gradual movement from disorder to order prefigures the possibilities of action for Odysseus, whose object must finally be to restore a lost order to his home and people.]

The *Odyssey*'s hierarchy is not the Aristotelian set of categories, much less Dante's perfectly calibrated realization of the distance separating utter chaos from absolute order, but comparisons are nevertheless viable. ⟨. . .⟩

There are ⟨. . .⟩ a series of mythic representations for the elements or elemental forces: Skylla, Charybdis, Proteus, Aiolos, and Helios' cattle. They have their laws which must be learned if Odysseus is to survive. Some, like Skylla, cannot be outwitted at all. Others can be outwitted by a prior knowledge of their cyclical pattern, as Odysseus turns Charybdis' schedule to his eventual advantage. ⟨. . .⟩

⟨T⟩here is a hierarchy from simple to complex, and the range of systems gives us something of Homer's idea of culture as measurable by the increasing complexity of social structures and by the degree of interaction between society and nature. At the lowest level are brutes like the Laistrygonians, but they need hardly detain us since in the Kyklopes, their next of kin in the evolutionary family, Homer has given a full portrait of the primitive. ⟨. . .⟩

To move from Polyphemos' cave to Kalypso's island is a distinct matriculation. ⟨. . .⟩ It is a carefully constructed ideal landscape set in concentric balance: trees, springs, meadow, cave, nymph. ⟨. . .⟩

The intelligence that begins to emerge in the character of Kalypso becomes yet more elaborated among the Phaiakians, whose behavior reflects the orderly disposition and the intricate harmonies of their palace and grounds. ⟨. . .⟩

When we turn our attention to Ithaka we understand the function of these prior documents of order, natural and human. Affairs in Ithaka are in complete disarray and the societies Odysseus passes through on his way home, and in a lesser way those his son visits at Pylos and Sparta, are paradigms for the restitution of order there. ⟨. . .⟩

The full landscape and architectural description is lacking when Odysseus arrives at his palace. Instead, it is transferred from Odysseus' arrival to Penelope's entrance into the storeroom in the inner recesses of the palace (note ἔσχατον, 21.9). That is the moment in Ithaka most directly comparable to Odysseus' arrival at Scheria. ⟨. . .⟩

Amid the wealth of oaken beams, gleaming doors, chests, and precious metals, the key, most unpretentious of objects, becomes imbued with extraordinary beauty and dignity. Now it is another token of the craftsmanship that once prevailed and is the object that provides access to the inner room which, together with its contents, has resisted the disintegration outside (vv. 6–7): "With resolute hand she grasped the well-carved key; beautiful it was, bronze, fitted with a handle of ivory." The most important of all objects within the chamber that key unlocks is the bow. When Odysseus handles it later he turns it this way and that, examining it with a practiced eye for possible termite damage in its owner's absence (21.393–400). But the chamber's sturdy structure and Eurykleia's faithful management have done their work well. What is stored in the chamber remains there undamaged. Preserved intact, the bow emerges from its hiding place, as its owner does from his, to become the pivotal object, not only memorial of the past order but the fatal instrument by which the old order is renewed.

—Norman Austin, *Archery at the Dark of the Moon: Poetic Problems in Homer's* Odyssey (Berkeley: University of California Press, 1975): pp. 132, 135, 143, 149, 157–58, 162, 170, 171.

PAOLO VIVANTE ON THE POETICS OF TIME

[Paolo Vivante is Professor Emeritus of Classics at McGill University, and author of *The Homeric Imagination: A Study of Homer's Poetic Perception of Reality* (1970) and *The* Iliad: *Action as Poetry* (1990). Here Vivante shows how, by assigning regularized expressions to recurring events (such as daybreak), Homer locates the events of his narrative in a continuous flow of time.]

⟨W⟩hat ultimately determines these basic variations is an inborn, keen realization of how such an event as day-break is actually seen in its happening—of how it affects a man or woman in the most concrete physical sense. The occurrence of day-break, in other words, is not abstracted from its actuality. It is not something to be designated one way or another for other reasons than those prompted by the event itself. The felicity of expression thus consists in congruity with reality. ⟨...⟩

We may again find a reason in Homer's sense of time—in the way the factual matter is reduced into concrete moments, into pure outlines of rest or movement. We have instances rather than facts. Take such ordinary recurring expressions as 'upon the laid-out victuals they put forth their hands', or 'they drew down the ships to the sea divine', or 'he bound the beautiful sandals under the glistening feet'. The moment is isolated and thus made typical by being keenly perceived. Time is the quickening element. It permeates the short sentences. It draws into its rhythm the noun-epithet phrases. What stands out is incidence, cadence. We have sequences and not informative details. It is as if the touch of time penetrated each thing, relieving it of its static objectivity. Hands and victuals, sea and ship, sandals and feet are all one with the vivid occasion: they are hardly necessary to the narrative, they fill our sense of the instant by drawing momentary relevance from the human act and conferring to it, in their turn, an existential concreteness. All this would not have been possible, if the facts had been accounted for in a general way (by saying, e.g., 'they ate and drank'), or if they had been described in detail (by giving us, e.g., an account of the victuals). Both general narrative and minute description would have been fatal to the momentary impact. But, as it is, we have time-filled instances, moments that come and go; we have rhythms and not a factual account.

Consider now this rendering of things on the voluminous Homeric scale, and see how it furthers a sense of what is typical. The recurring phrases compose the existential texture of the action. They attach any episode to its indispensable phases, to its vantage-points of duration. The recurrence of phrase thus reflects the recurrence of acts which mark basic points of succession. On the other hand, these recurrences naturally take a typical form. Hence a sense of what is typical springing from the perception of life. Hence a stylization which is continually sustained by a sense of developing outlines in the actuality of events. There is hardly any matter in the poems that seems exempt from this treatment. Like day-break and night-fall, human activities have their rising and setting. ⟨. . .⟩

Try to visualize a complex enduring event, and you can only see it in a series of instances which typify it. Hence in the *Iliad* the fighting scenes which rehearse the same event time after time. Homer carries out this process on a vast poetic level. His practice is to visualize rather than describe, summarize, idealize, dream, glorify, moralize.

—Paolo Vivante, "Rose-Fingered Dawn and the Idea of Time," *Ramus* 8, no. 2 (1979): pp. 130, 134–35.

[Rainer Friedrich is a professor of Classics at Dalhousie University, and author of *Stilwandel im homerischen Epos* (1975). In "On the Compositional Use of Similes in the *Odyssey*" (1981), Friedrich analyzes the lion imagery of the *Iliad* and contrasts it with similes in Books VI and XXII of the *Odyssey*. This extract highlights the ambivalence of the *Odyssey*'s attitude toward heroic violence, and links it with Odysseus' refusal to revel in the triumph over the Suitors ("To glory over slain men is no piety," he says in Book XXII, line 462).]

Embodying noble daring and energetic strength as well as ferocity of attack and the recklessness of determined prowess, the lion stands out among the other animals used in similes of the *Iliad*; occasionally, the wild boar or a bird of prey may replace him. In fact, the lion stands out in the same way in which the great heroes are distinguished from the rank and file which all too often are reduced to providing the corpses in a hero's ἀριστεία. The heroic animal *par excellence.* ⟨. . .⟩ Thus the lion simile not only illustrates, it also glorifies. ⟨. . .⟩

This simile ⟨in *Od.* 6.130 ff.⟩ clearly echos the simile of *Il.* 12.299 and invites comparison. In both similes a λέων ὀρεσίτροφος—an *epitheton significans*, not *ornans*!—is driven by hunger from his accustomed hunting grounds in the mountains where his usual prey is—wild animals, the larger cattle which graze in the wilderness, and the occasional strayed sheep; he approaches human settlements to go after the smaller livestock which remain close to the farm. But this is as far as the similarity goes. In the *Iliad* simile, this is only the opening; the lion then attacks, meets with resistance by armed men with dogs; but he sustains his attack regardless of the danger. The lion of this simile, although driven by hunger, remains every inch the ἀλκιμώτατον ζῷον of the traditional lion simile. It is the lion's spirited attack and his courageous determination on which the simile turns—in accordance with the heroic action of the narrative it describes. The *Odyssey* simile, however, has as its main theme what in the *Iliad* simile is only the introductory situation: it elaborates the condition of a living being which, exposed to the natural elements, is driven by sheer need (γαστήρ, χρειώ) from the wilderness to civilized regions. ⟨. . .⟩

In *Od.* 22.401 the lion simile, unlike the one in Bk. 6, seems to be found in its traditional context, the battle scene: it marks the end of Odysseus' fight with the suitors, his ἀριστεία. However, there is a significant displacement. Instead of describing and glorifying Odysseus' heroic deeds *during* this ἀριστεία, or his warlike spirit *prior* to it—the traditional placement of the beast-of-prey simile in the *Iliad*—this lion simile is placed right *after* the fight with the suitors. Moreover, like the lion simile in Bk. 6, it concentrates on physical appearance—this time the physical appearance of hero and lion after committing a slaughterous act.

Now, gory details such as the devouring of the victim's blood and entrails are also found in lion similes of the *Iliad*; but only as part of a broader picture which emphasizes the heroic splendour of lion and warrior. This *Odyssey* simile, however, concentrates *exclusively* on the abhorrent view of a blood-spattered lion after his terrible meal. By making this the sole object of the simile, the *Odyssey* poet— instead of glorifying the lion as the ἀλκιμώτατον ζῷον—seems to disparage the animal for its savagery. What such an ambiguous image may imply for the understanding of the μνηστηροφονία will have to be discussed later. At any rate, in this lion simile of the *Odyssey* the prototype of noble daring has become a slaughterous beast. ⟨. . .⟩

Should one conclude that the simile implies a critical judgment on Odysseus' deed, the slaying of the suitors? Certainly, such a conclusion would overstate the case: the necessity of this deed is never in doubt. Nevertheless, there is a profound ambiguity about Odysseus' ἀριστεία—an ambiguity which lies in its nature and of which the hero himself seems to be aware. ⟨. . .⟩

Odysseus' prohibiting Eurycleia from raising the cry of triumph over the slain suitors points to the problematical nature of his ἀριστεία. It is, after all, not taking place in a war between enemies, but is rather the expression of the inner strife of a community in which the king is pitted against the hybristic nobility of his own country in mortal combat. It ends in the wholesale slaughter of the ἄριστοι κούρων—a result not to be glorified as a μέγα ἔργον, however glorious the returning hero's fight and victory may have been. Gone is the innocent and spontaneous delight in fighting and killing which can be felt in the unproblematical ἀριστεῖαι of the *Iliad*.

—Rainer Friedrich, "On the Compositional Use of Similes in the *Odyssey*," *American Journal of Philology* 102, no. 2 (Summer, 1981): pp. 120–21, 122–23, 124–25, 129, 130–31.

JOHN PERADOTTO ON NO-MAN AND EVERYMAN

[John Peradotto is Andrew V. Raymond Chair of Classics at the State University of New York, Buffalo, and editor of *Women in the Ancient World: The Arethusa Papers* (1984). In this extract from *Man in the Middle Voice* (1990), he considers the ambiguity of Odysseus' names (*polytropos* suggesting both "much-turning" and "much-turned," *odyssamenos* suggesting both "hating" and "hated"), relating it to the new sense of the self that arises with the character and poem.]

To what does the name "Odysseus" refer? ⟨. . .⟩ In the long run, what identifying description will serve more reliably than the *Odyssey* itself? For the poem sustains without final resolution an alternation between myth and *Märchen*, between the narrative of desire frustrated and the narrative of desire fulfilled, between the story of a versatile agent and the story of an enduring patient. That alternation has its analogue in the tension within the hero's names—*polytropos* 'much-turning' and 'much-turned,' *odyssamenos* 'hating' and 'hated'—and in the tension between his names—*ptoliporthios* versus Outis, *polymēchanos* versus *polytlas*, the last two epithets used of him. Nowhere are the contending Bakhtinian voices more evident than in the closing lines of the poem, where these two epithets are ranged ironically against one another: Odysseus is called *polytlas* (24.537), the epithet suggesting endurance in the face of the inevitable, at the very moment when, active master of the situation, he launches into action; he is called *polymētis* (24.542), suggesting control of the world by infinite cunning, in the context of its curtailment (ἴσχεο, παῦε, 543) as it confronts its limits.

To what does the name "Odysseus" refer? In a sense, it refers to a broadened sense of the self. In comparison with the *Iliad*, the *Odyssey* seems to present a paradigm of human potential that is considerably less deterministic. Instead of the narrow quest for an abiding *kleos* beyond death, that attempt permanently to fix the name in the community through competitive excellence, the poet's realization of his capacity to predicate nearly anything of his subject creates a "character" of infinite variety, whose self-chosen anonymity, identified with *mētis*, becomes a paradigm, when taken over into "real life," for a subtler ideology of the self still embryonic in the *Iliad*, a sense of self with depth. In the self-consciousness of his art, the storyteller creates a subject at once *polytropos* and *outis*, a secret base for open predication, rather than a determinate sum of predicates, and thus presents a paradigm for a view of the self as capable, dynamic, free, rather than fixed, fated, defined. ⟨. . .⟩

To what does the name "Odysseus" refer? In the final analysis, it refers in a sense to no one, to nothing, but nothing in the rich sense of the zero-degree, which signifies not simply nonbeing, but potentiality, what it means for the empty subject of narrative to take on any predication or attribute, for Athena to simulate anyone (13.313), for dormant Proteus to become anything that is, for Outis to become *polytropos*. It is the point where Sisyphus, true progenitor of Odysseus, unlike his immobilized companions Tityus and Tantalus, rebounds against failure, forever resilient even in the realm of death to face Krataiis, the ruthless power of necessity. It is the zero-point where every story begins, the zero-point where every story ends, rich with the possibility of another beginning.

> —John Peradotto, *Man in the Middle Voice: Name and Narration in the* Odyssey (Princeton: Princeton University Press, 1990): pp. 168–69, 170.

ANDREW FORD ON POETRY AND BELATEDNESS

[Andrew Ford is an associate professor of Classics at Princeton University. In this extract from *Homer: The Poetry of the Past* (1992), he explains how the *Iliad* and *Odyssey* orient themselves differently in relation to both the present and the past.]

The *Iliad* for the most part dismisses any thought of itself as performance in order to present the deeds as unfolding "now." ⟨...⟩ Achilles sings in his tent about the deeds of former men, but his own glory has yet to be achieved. "For a long time, I think the Achaeans will remember our strife," he says in reconciling with Agamemnon, but this remembrance will arise in the future, and it is not clear what form it will take. ⟨...⟩ Helen is more self-conscious and, when we first see her, has begun to put "the many Struggles of the Achaeans and the Trojans" into a tapestry. But again the main action of the war and the poem remains to be done, and she breaks off her weaving to go and look at the army from the city wall. In a much-noted speech she says more than Achilles about fame, that this war for her sake will be *sung* about; but again, this will be in later generations, "among men to come." ⟨...⟩

Though not without its ironic moments of self-reference then, the *Iliad* takes a very austere stance toward its audience. It almost completely effaces itself as performance and postpones its coming into shape to the end. By this resolute self-repression it achieves a vivid presence in which the focus is kept on the actors in their acting. The *Odyssey* has a different stance toward song and achieves a different kind of vividness. It sees a longer history of singing behind it and portrays itself consciously as the last in a long line of song. Even before Troy a song of the *Argo* was on the lips of all (12.70). Its own characters, both the living and the recently dead, are already enshrined in Trojan songs whose fame has reached heaven; the poetry of the returns is already arising. It is in this song-filled world that Odysseus must find a place for his own fame. The *Odyssey*, then, decides to offer not the deed before the song but the newest in a long line of songs. Its poetic is summed up by its hero, who concludes his performance by saying "It is hateful for me to tell once again what has already been clearly told" (12.452–453). ⟨...⟩

By retrojecting song, the *Odyssey* poet makes his song early, makes it come straight from the horse's mouth, as he speaks it. If the *Iliad* banishes itself to get a direct vision of the heroic world, the *Odyssey* retrojects itself into that world, so that performance is no longer a late thing, after the event, but one involved with it and in part preceding it. The differences between the stances of the two poems toward their own past may be summarized. The *Iliad* sees itself as song to come; it values action over representation, deeds over boasts, as Aenèas values fighting over rehearsing genealogies in book 22. ⟨. . .⟩

In the *Iliad* action is taking place under the eyes of the gods, who will make it song, but under our eyes too. In the *Odyssey* we witness not only heroic deeds but early singing about those deeds, as both poem and hero wander toward their final destination. Song is very much a part of this early world, and so even as we listen to our bard, we are playing the part of heroes.

—Andrew Ford, *Homer: The Poetry of the Past* (Ithaca: Cornell University Press, 1992): pp. 127–28, 129, 130.

Works by
Homer

Greek texts:

Opera. Ed. Demetrios Chalkokondyles, 1488.

Odysseia. Ed. Aldo Pio Manuzio, 1504.

Ilias et Odyssea. Ed. J. Micyllus, 1541.

Works. Eds. Jacobus Micyllus and Joachim Camerarius, 1541.

Ilias. Ed. Ioannis Crespini Atrebatii, 1559.

Ilias. Ed. Johann Guenther, 1563.

Ilias. Ed. Georgius Bishop, 1591.

Opera. Ed. Johannes Field, 1660.

Ilias. Ed. Johannes Hayes, 1679.

Ilias. Ed. Thomas Day Seymour, 1695.

Opera. Ed. Samuel Clarke, 1740.

Works. Eds. Thomas Grenville, Richard Porson, et al., 1800.

Ilias et Odyssea. Ed. Richard Payne Knight, 1820.

Works. Ed. Wilhelm Dindorf, 1828.

Odyssey. Ed. Henry Hayman, 1882.

Odyssea. Ed. Arthur Ludwich, 1890.

Ilias. Ed. Dominicus Comparetti, 1901.

Opera. Eds. David B. Monro and Thomas W. Allen, 1912.

Odyssey. Ed. A. T. Murray, 1919.

Ilias et Odyssea. Ed. Eduardi Schwartz, 1924.

Odyssey. Ed. W. B. Stanford, 1948.

Odyssea. Ed. Helmut van Thiel, 1991.

Translations into English:

The Whole Works of Homer. Trans. George Chapman, 1612.

Odyssey. Trans. John Ogilby, 1659.

Iliad. Trans. John Ogilby, 1660.

The Iliad and Odyssey of Homer. Trans. Thomas Hobbes, 1673.

The Iliad of Homer. Trans. Alexander Pope, 1720.

The Odyssey of Homer. Trans. Alexander Pope, William Broome, and Elijah Fenton, 1726.

The Iliad of Homer. Trans. James Macpherson, 1773.

The Iliad and Odyssey of Homer. Trans. William Cowper, 1791.

The Iliad of Homer. Trans. William Cullen Bryant, 1870.

The Odyssey of Homer. Trans. William Cullen Bryant, 1872.

The Odyssey of Homer. Trans. S. H. Butcher and Andrew Lang, 1879.

Iliad. Trans. Andrew Lang, Walter Leaf, and Ernest Myers, 1883.

The Odyssey of Homer. Trans. William Morris, 1887.

The Odyssey of Homer. Trans. George Herbert Palmer, 1891.

The Odyssey of Homer. Trans. Samuel Butler, 1900.

The Iliad of Homer. Trans. Samuel Butler, 1898.

Iliad. Trans. A. T. Murray, 1924.

Odyssey. Trans. A. T. Murray, 1931.

The Odyssey of Homer. Trans. T. E. Lawrence, 1932.

Iliad. Trans. W. H. D. Rouse, 1937.

The Story of Odysseus. Trans. W. H. D. Rouse, 1942.

Iliad. Trans. Richmond Lattimore, 1951.

Odyssey. Trans. Robert Fitzgerald, 1961.

Odyssey. Trans. Richmond Lattimore, 1967.

Iliad. Trans. Robert Fitzgerald, 1974.

Works about
Homer

Allen, Walter, Jr. "The Theme of the Suitors in the *Odyssey.*" *Transactions and Proceedings of the American Philological Association* 70 (1939): 104–24.

Aristotle. *Poetics.* Trans. S. H. Butcher. London: St. Martin's Press, 1894.

Austin, Norman. *Archery at the Dark of the Moon: Poetic Problems in Homer's* Odyssey. Berkeley: University of California Press, 1975.

Becker, Andrew Sprague. *The Shield of Achilles and the Poetry of Ekphrasis.* London: Rowman and Littlefield, 1995.

Bespaloff, Rachel. *On the* Iliad. Washington: Bollingen, 1947.

Bowra, C. M. *Tradition and Design in the* Iliad. Oxford: Clarendon Press, 1930.

Bradford, Ernle. *Ulysses Found.* New York: Harcourt, Brace, 1963.

Byre, Calvin S. "Penelope and the Suitors Before Odysseus: *Odyssey* 18.158–303." *American Journal of Philology* 109 (1988): 159–173.

Carpenter, Rhys. *Folk Tale, Fiction and Saga in the Homeric Epics.* Berkeley: University of California Press, 1946.

Clay, Jenny Strauss. *The Wrath of Athena: Gods and Men in the* Odyssey. Princeton: Princeton University Press, 1983.

D'Arms, Edward F. and Karl K. Hulley. "The Oresteia-Story in the *Odyssey.*" *Transactions of the American Philological Association* 77 (1946): 207–13.

Davies, Malcolm. "The Judgement of Paris and Iliad Book XXIV." *Journal of Hellenic Studies* 101 (1981): 56–62.

De Jong, Irene J. F. *Homer: Critical Assessments.* 4 vols. London: Routledge, 1999.

Dodds, E. R. *The Greeks and the Irrational.* Berkeley: University of California Press, 1951.

Emlyn-Jones, Chris. "True and Lying Tales in the *Odyssey.*" *Greece and Rome* 33 (1986): 1–10.

Fenik, Bernard. "Typical Battle Scenes in the *Iliad*: Studies in the Narrative Techniques of Homeric Battle Description." *Hermes,* suppl. 21 (1968).

Ford, Andrew. *Homer: The Poetry of the Past*. Ithaca: Cornell University Press, 1962.

Frame, Douglas. *The Myth of Return in Early Greek Epic*. New Haven: Yale University Press, 1978.

Griffin, Jasper. *Homer on Life and Death*. Oxford: Clarendon Press, 1980.

Harsh, Philip Whaley. "Penelope and Odysseus in *Odyssey* XIX." *American Journal of Philology* 71 (1950): 1–21.

Havelock, Eric A. *Preface to Plato*. Cambridge: Harvard University Press, 1963.

Kirk, G. S., ed. *The Language and Background of Homer: Some Recent Studies and Controversies*. Cambridge: Heffer, 1964.

Lord, Albert B. *The Singer of Tales*. Cambridge: Harvard University Press, 1960.

Mueller, Martin. *The Iliad*. London: George Allen and Unwin, 1984.

Murray, Gilbert. *The Rise of the Greek Epic*. New York: Oxford University Press, 1960.

Myres, J. L. "The Last Book of the 'Iliad': Its Place in the Structure of the Poem." *Journal of Hellenic Studies* 52 (1932): 264–96.

Nagler, Michael N. *Spontaneity and Tradition: A Study in the Oral Art of Homer*. Berkeley: University of California Press, 1974.

Nagy, Gregory. *The Best of the Achaeans: Concepts of the Hero in Archaic Greek Poetry*. Baltimore: Johns Hopkins University Press, 1979.

Nilsson, Martin P. *Homer and Mycenae*. London: Methuen, 1933.

Otto, Walter F. *The Homeric Gods*. Trans. Moses Hadas. New York: Pantheon, 1954.

Page, Denys L. *History and the Homeric* Iliad. Berkeley: University of California Press, 1959.

Parry, Anne Amory. "Blameless Aegisthus: A Study of AMYMΩN and Other Homeric Epithets." *Mnemosyne,* suppl. 26 (1973).

Parry, Milman. *The Making of Homeric Verse*. Ed. Adam Parry. Oxford: Clarendon Press, 1971.

Porter, David H. "Violent Juxtaposition in the Similes of the *Iliad.*" *Classical Journal* 68 (1972): 11–21.

Powell, Barry B. *Composition by Theme in the* Odyssey. Meisenheim am Glan: Anton Hain, 1977.

Pucci, Pietro. *Odysseus Polutropos: Intertextual Readings in the* Odyssey *and the* Iliad. Ithaca: Cornell University Press, 1987.

Redfield, James M. *Nature and Culture in the* Iliad: *The Tragedy of Hector.* Durham: Duke University Press, 1994.

Rubino, Carl A. and Cynthia W. Shelmerdine. *Approaches to Homer.* Austin: University of Texas Press, 1983.

Scully, Stephen. "Doubling in the Tale of Odysseus." *Classical World* 80 (1987): 401–17.

Segal, Charles. "The Theme of the Mutilation of the Corpse in the *Iliad.*" *Mnemosyne,* suppl. 17 (1971).

Sheppard, J. T. *The Pattern of the* Iliad. New York: Haskell, 1966.

Stanford, W. B. *The Ulysses Theme: A Study in the Adaptability of a Traditional Hero.* Oxford: Basil Blackwell, 1954.

Taylor, Charles A., Jr., ed. *Essays on the* Odyssey: *Selected Modern Criticism.* Bloomington: Indiana University Press, 1963.

Thornton, Agathe. *People and Themes in Homer's* Odyssey. London: Methuen, 1970.

Vivante, Paolo. "Homer and the Aesthetic Moment." *Arion* 4 (1965): 415–38.

Wace, Alan J. B., ed. *A Companion to Homer.* New York: Macmillan, 1962.

Weil, Simone. *The* Iliad *or the Poem of Force.* Trans. Mary McCarthy. Wallingford: Pendle Hill, 1956.

Whitman, Cedric H. *Homer and the Heroic Tradition.* Cambridge, Mass.: Harvard University Press, 1958.

Woolsey, Robert B. "Repeated Narratives in the *Odyssey.*" *Classical Philology* 36 (1941): 167–81.

Wright, G. M. and P. V. Jones, eds. *Homer: German Scholarship in Translation.* Oxford: Clarendon Press, 1997.

Index of
Themes and Ideas